First published in 2004 by New Holland Publishers (UK) Ltd
London • Cape Town • Sydney • Auckland
Garfield House, 86–88 Edgware Road, London W2 2EA, United Kingdom
www.newhollandpublishers.com
80 McKenzie Street, Cape Town 8001, South Africa
Unit 1, 66 Gibbes Street, Chatswood, NSW 2067, Australia
218 Lake Road, Northcote, Auckland, New Zealand

ISBN 978 1 84330 544 6
10 9 8 7 6

Editorial Direction: Rosemary Wilkinson Senior Editor: Clare Hubbard Production: Hazel Kirkman
Designed and created for New Holland by AG&G Books Copyright © 2004 "Specialist" AG&G Books
Design: Glyn Bridgewater Illustrations: Dawn Brend, Gill Bridgewater and Coral Mula Editor: Alison Copland
Photographs: AG&G Books (pages 10–11 and 12), Jonathan Clark, Gandy's (Roses) Ltd, www.gandys-
roses.co.uk (cover front and pages 2 and 54CR), Garden Matters (pages 25CL, 47TR, 60CR, 61BR, 66CL,
68CR, 70CL and 72CL), Peter McHoy (page 52BL) and David Squire (all pictures except those listed here).
Reproduction by Pica Digital Pte Ltd, Singapore
Printed and bound in Malaysia by Times Offset (M) Sdn. Bhd.

The PRUNING

KU-545-619

The essential guide to caring for shrubs, trees, climbers, hedges, conifers, roses and fruit trees

David Squire

Series editors: A. & G. Bridgewater

NEW HOLLAND

Contents

Author's foreword 2

Author's foreword

Gardeners are shapers of the environment, seldom being content to leave the growth of plants – from shrubs and trees to climbers and hedges – to the seasonal whims of nature. They are also forgers of better ways to grow plants, perhaps to improve their fruiting qualities or to be able to grow them in space-restricted areas or cold environments. Cordon apples and pears, as well as espaliers, can be grown in relatively narrow beds alongside paths, while in cool areas fan-trained peaches and nectarines have a greater chance of success than if planted as bushes in the middle of an exposed garden.

In temperate climates, it is the coldness of winter that limits the seasonal growth of plants and gives an indication of the best time to get out secateurs and other pruning equipment. Some plants can be pruned during their dormant period, while others need to have their sap starting to move in early spring before they can be safely pruned. Conversely, some plants 'bleed' when radically pruned in summer.

Throughout this abundantly illustrated and thoroughly practical book, advice is given about pruning garden plants, from infancy to maturity. There is even detailed advice about renovating neglected plants, from shrubs and climbers to fruit trees and bushes, should an untidy and unloved garden be inherited. There is also a fun element, with instructions about introducing topiary into your garden; few gardeners can resist the possibility of owning a topiary-created bird.

SEASONS

Throughout this book, advice is given about the best times to prune plants. Because of global and even regional variations in climate and temperature, the four main seasons have been used, with each subdivided into 'early', 'mid-' and 'late' – for example, early spring, mid-spring and late spring. These 12 divisions of the year can be applied to the appropriate calendar months in your local area, if you find this helps. In some northerly areas, spring may begin several weeks later than in more southerly regions.

Measurements

Both metric and imperial measurements are given in this book – for example, 1.8 m (6 ft).

What is pruning?

A clinical but nevertheless accurate definition of pruning would be: the removal of parts of a woody plant to train and shape it, maintain good health and, for many plants, achieve a balance between growth and flowering. Pruning is also used to improve the quality of fruits, flowers, leaves and stems. Too often, it is employed just to limit the growth of a plant, such as when pollarding trees in space-restricted areas.

Is pruning my plants essential?

MAINTAINING PLANT HEALTH

Plants that are pruned each year – whether radically or just to check them over – will inevitably be healthier than those that are neglected. Diseases and pests soon wreak havoc in plants and it is advisable to regularly cut out infected parts. If left, infection will spread and can cause entire branches to die. Dead shoots are also unsightly, especially when they remain on ornamental shrubs, trees and climbers.

Cut out shoots infected by fireblight to about 60 cm (2 ft) beyond the damaged area.

BALANCING GROWTH AND FLOWERING

For many flowering shrubs, pruning helps to create a balance between growth and the production of flowers. During a plant's early years, pruning is for training and for shoot and branch formation. Later, it is to ensure that growth is not at the expense of flowers. It is a delicate balance, as heavy and severe pruning can prevent or delay flower development. Getting this balance right is essential.

QUALITY IMPROVEMENTS

Humulus lupulus 'Aureus' dies down in autumn; cut out all the stems.

Regular pruning helps to improve the quality and size of flowers, fruits, leaves and stems. The size and quality of flowers on the late summer-flowering shrub *Buddleja davidii* (Butterfly Bush) diminishes when pruning is neglected, while cane, bush and tree fruits also deteriorate; with each year there is an increase in the number of old stems. Decorative shrubs (such as Dogwoods), which have colourful stems during winter, will not create a good display if pruning is neglected, while some shrubs (such as *Sambucus racemosa* 'Plumosa Aurea' and *Sambucus nigra* 'Aurea') produce young and attractive foliage if severely pruned each year.

This shaped Buxus sempervirens 'Suffruticosa' needs to be clipped regularly throughout summer in order to keep it looking neat.

Azaleas create a magnificent display in spring and into early summer. They need little regular pruning, other than occasionally cutting out congested shoots after the flowers fade.

Philosophy of pruning

Which plants need pruning?

Pruning is a gardening skill too often cloaked in magic and mystery, whereas in practice it is a logical process that is easy to understand and to apply to plants. It is mainly performed on woody plants, ranging from ornamental trees, shrubs and climbers to fruit trees and bushes. Roses are other popular candidates, together with hedges which need attention during their formative years as well as throughout their lives.

THE RANGE OF PLANTS THAT BENEFIT FROM PRUNING

Flowering shrubs
Flowering shrubs, from *Forsythia* to *Weigela*, usually need yearly pruning to encourage the regular production of flowers.

Ornamental trees
Ornamental trees invariably need less pruning than shrubs, but it is essential during their early years to create a strong framework of branches.

Roses
All roses need yearly pruning, regardless of whether they are bush types (Hybrid Teas and Floribundas), climbers, ramblers or standards.

Hedges
Hedges, from those grown for their attractive leaves to ones that become smothered in flowers, all need regular pruning.

Tree fruits
Tree fruits, such as apples, pears, plums and peaches, need careful pruning during their infancy to create a strong and well-spaced framework of branches.

Bush and cane fruits
Bush and cane fruits, ranging from blackcurrants to raspberries, require yearly pruning to encourage the regular production of fruits.

This pretty garden includes many types of plant – such as trees, climbers and shrubs – that need pruning to help them grow well and look good.

WHY PRUNE PLANTS?

If woody plants – from shrubs and climbers to fruit trees and bushes – are neglected, they become unsightly and unproductive. Additionally, their life-spans are shortened and they become havens of delight for pests and diseases.

Pruning is essential for most plants, although some, such as the evergreen *Aucuba japonica* 'Variegata' (Spotted Laurel), create spectacular features each year with no regular pruning. However, *Philadelphus* (Mock Orange) can soon become an entanglement of old, non-flowering stems if yearly pruning is neglected.

Some shrubs, such as *Sambucus racemosa* 'Plumosa Aurea' and *Sambucus nigra* 'Aurea', are grown for their attractive young foliage, which is produced by cutting all stems right down to ground level in late winter or early spring. Without this severe treatment, these shrubs would not be nearly so attractive. Some *Rhus* species, including *Rhus typhina* 'Dissecta', can be treated in the same way.

Changing climates

With the advent of global warming, the seasonal influence of winter – which dictates when many plants are pruned – may change. Traditionally, shrubs that flower during late summer and into autumn are not pruned until late winter or early spring. This is because, if they were pruned as soon as their flowers faded, any young, tender shoots that subsequently developed would be damaged by frost. Even now in some areas the late-flowering *Buddleja davidii* (Butterfly Bush) can be pruned in autumn, rather than at the traditional time in spring. Even if a few young shoots of this shrub are damaged by early frosts, there are others to replace them.

It is impossible to suggest with any certainty what the pattern of weather will be in a couple of decades' time, but gardeners will have to take a flexible attitude at least to the pruning of late-flowering shrubs, which are normally pruned in spring.

GETTING THE TIMING RIGHT

It is the influence of a cold period within the yearly cycle of a plant's growth that mainly influences the time when it is pruned. For example, woody-framed plants such as apples and pears are pruned during winter when they are dormant. At that time, as well as being inactive, they are free from leaves and fruits and the tree's structure can be clearly seen.

Flowering shrubs have a different nature and pruning is dictated both by the season when the shrub produces its flowers and the cold period in its yearly cycle of growth. For example, shrubs such as *Forsythia* that flower early in the year can be pruned as soon as their flowers fade. There is then sufficient time for new shoots to develop and to mature before the onset of harsh winter weather. However, those shrubs that flower late in summer have their pruning left

until spring. If they were pruned as soon as their flowers faded, their newly developing shoots would be damaged by winter weather. For example, *Fuchsia magellanica* flowers from mid-summer to mid-autumn and is pruned in spring, when young growth will not be damaged.

Deciduous Magnolias resent pruning; wounds do not heal.

This beautiful display, which includes flowering and foliage shrubs as well as climbing roses and other climbers, needs regular pruning to ensure that it creates a spectacular feature each year.

Avoiding pruning problems

Trees with sappy wood, such as *Aesculus* (Horse Chestnuts), *Betula* (Birches), conifers and some Maples (*Acer*), are likely to bleed if cut during summer when their sap is flowing strongly. Therefore, they are best pruned in late autumn or early winter.

Most ornamental and fruiting trees are pruned during their dormant period. However, nectarines, peaches, cherries, plums and gages are especially susceptible to bacterial canker and silver leaf disease when cuts are made during their dormant period. Therefore, wait until their sap is rising in spring.

CHANGING STYLES OF ROSE PRUNING

For many years, the pruning of bush roses such as Hybrid Teas and Floribundas has involved secateurs. To many gardeners, this is an essential facet of growing roses each year to produce the best quality and number of flowers. However, experiments in pruning bush roses have involved using electric hedge-trimmers to cut down all stems, with cuts being made irrespective of their positions. Some surprisingly good results have been achieved in this way, but for most gardeners the traditional way of individually pruning bush roses gives greater satisfaction and involvement.

PRUNING DOS AND DON'TS

Do:

✔ Ensure that all pruning equipment is sharp and will make clean cuts in the desired position.

✔ Keep pruning equipment clean. After use, wash and dry all surfaces, and thinly wipe the blades with oil.

✔ Pick up and burn all prunings, especially those showing signs of disease or pest damage.

✔ Wear strong gloves when pruning roses and other plants with thorns or sharp stems.

✔ Stand on the ground to prune plants; old boxes and stools can quickly slip from underneath you.

Don't:

✘ Use a pruning knife unless you are proficient with it. They soon cause accidents when used by novice pruners.

✘ Try to cut thick stems with secateurs that are insufficiently large – they bend and become distorted.

✘ Use a mains-powered hedge-trimmer or chainsaw unless a power-breaking device is installed in the circuit. Should a cable inadvertently be cut, this device instantly cuts off the power supply.

✘ Treat saws, secateurs and powered cutters carelessly – they can cut off fingers as well as twigs.

Plant groups and treatments

Many garden plants benefit from pruning, ranging from shrubs and climbers to apples and raspberries. Here is a broad idea of them, together with the principles of their treatment. Some fruiting types, such as trees and grape vines, have two distinct pruning stages in their lives. The first stage encompasses their formative years, when their structure is being developed; the second stage is when they are established and regularly producing fruits.

What are the benefits of pruning?

LARGE TREES

If, with a new garden, you have inherited a large tree – perhaps an Oak, Ash or Beech – it is more than likely that it has been neglected for many years. These are magnificent trees and if not checked regularly may deteriorate. Heavy snowfalls and strong winds break branches, and unless removed they could be dangerous to you and your neighbours. Some large branches can be cut off in stages (see page 9), but for very large trees it is safer to call in a professional tree surgeon rather than tackle the job yourself.

Snow tapping

Damage from snow falling on evergreen shrubs can be reduced by using a Bamboo cane to lightly tap the stems to dislodge snow before it freezes. Take care not to damage leaves.

BAMBOO CARE

Heavy falls of snow devastate Bamboos, bending canes at ground level and breaking or distorting them. If left, those that are bent may not recover and the only solution is to cut them down to ground level. However, if the snow can be removed quickly, before it freezes on the leaves, there is every possibility that the canes will recover within a few weeks.

Incidentally, wear strong gloves when handling the canes as many, when split, have sharp, razor-like edges that soon cut hands.

Ornamental shrubs

Weigela

Shrubs introduce a wider range of flowers than trees and many have a compact nature that suits small gardens. Some flowering shrubs, like *Mahonia* 'Charity' (Holly Grape), flower in winter, while others such as *Magnolia stellata* bloom in spring. Additionally, *Hibiscus syriacus* and *Hydrangea paniculata* 'Grandiflora' create magnificent displays in late summer.

Many shrubs have coloured or variegated leaves, while others reveal their glory in berries, such as *Callicarpa bodinieri* var. *giraldii* (Beauty Bush), Pyracanthas and *Gaultheria mucronata*.

Shrubs usually need more pruning than trees, and for flowering types this is indicated by the season in which they bear flowers (see pages 14–15 for advice on pruning these shrubs).

Ornamental trees

Prunus 'Kanzan'

These are varied and include flowering trees such as spring-flowering Cherry trees and early summer-flowering Laburnums. There are also trees with beautifully coloured foliage; a good example is *Gleditsia triacanthos* 'Sunburst', with yellow leaves. Then there are trees with coloured bark, including *Acer griseum* (Paperbark Maple), *Acer pensylvanicum* (Snakebark Maple) and *Betula papyrifera* (Paper Birch or Canoe Birch), with superbly coloured bark that will create interest throughout the year. Additionally, some trees have berries that bring welcome colour to winter, which can be a dull period.

Few of these trees need regular pruning, other than ensuring that branches are not damaged by strong wind or heavy snowfalls. Always make pruning repairs as soon as possible.

Climbers

Clematis 'Nelly Moser'

These are especially welcome in gardens as they not only create interest through their flowers and leaves but also provide seclusion and privacy. Some climbers have a natural tendency to climb, while others, such as *Jasminum nudiflorum* (Winter-flowering Jasmine), are nature's leaners. Ivies, of course, have no hesitation to all but glue themselves to walls and to scale great heights.

Pruning many of the climbers that are regularly seen in gardens is described on pages 18–39.

Do not think of climbers as being solely for scaling boundaries and house walls; by constructing a free-standing trellis about 2.1 m (7 ft) high and positioning it 75–90 cm (2½–3 ft) from a boundary fence it is possible to create greater privacy.

Fruit

Apple

The range of fruit that can be grown in a garden is wide, from apples and pears to soft fruits such as raspberries. Grapes are another possibility. Although these fruits are grown in quite different ways – from bushes and trees to canes and as climbers – they all need regular and special pruning (see pages 62–77).

In many areas, birds soon destroy fruit buds, causing irreparable damage. Therefore, in such circumstances it is best to choose relatively low forms and to grow them in a wire cage that is 2.4–3 m (8–10 ft) high. Although initially expensive, this is the best, long-term solution to a bird problem. If the problem is neglected, both growth and flowering will be decimated by birds in a short space of time.

Hedges

Ligustrum ovalifolium

Many shrubs can be used to form hedges. These range from the ubiquitous but reliable *Ligustrum ovalifolium* (Privet), in both its all-green and yellow-leaved forms, to flowering types. Some hedges have a rural nature and are often formed of a medley of wayside plants, while others are more formal and perhaps produced from a stately conifer such as *Taxus baccata* (Yew). With all hedges, it is especially important to encourage them to have a leaf-clad base (see pages 40–43).

As well as creating privacy, hedges are especially beneficial in windy and exposed areas, where they help to reduce the damaging nature of strong, blustery winds.

Roses

Rose (Hybrid Tea)

Few gardens do not have a rose bush, climber or rambler; all of them benefit from regular pruning to remain healthy and to produce a good display of flowers. Pruning roses is described in detail on pages 50–61, and this involves Hybrid Tea, Floribunda, rambler, climber, standard, pillar and shrub types. Each of these groups demands special pruning.

Most gardeners grow their bush roses primarily for garden display, but there is always an opportunity to cut a few blooms for room decoration. To avoid causing any long-term harm to bushes when cutting off some of their blooms for indoor display, do not cut off more than one-third of a flower's stem. Always cut to just above an outward-facing bud.

Stooling

Cornus alba (Dogwood)

Stooling means cutting a shrub right down to encourage the development of new shoots from its base. Several shrubs can be stooled each year to produce colourful stems (see page 15). Stooling can also be used as an easy and inexpensive way of increasing plants. For example, young shoots produced by stooling can be used when grafting apples and pears. Also, you can cut down shrubs such as Dogwoods to within 7.5 cm (3 in) of the ground in late winter, and, when new shoots are about 20 cm (8 in) high, mound soil over them. In the following late winter, remove the soil and sever the new plants from the parent. Plant them into a nursery bed or a border.

PRUNING FOR EXHIBITION PURPOSES

Some shrubs – especially those that flower late in summer on shoots produced earlier in the same season – can be encouraged to develop extra large flowerheads. For example, *Hydrangea paniculata* 'Grandiflora' has shoots normally pruned back by half, but if more severely pruned (by two-thirds) larger flowers are produced. Unfortunately, if this radical pruning is repeated for several years the life-span of the shrub is decreased.

Tackling neglected gardens

Can I renovate my garden?

Overgrown gardens can usually be renovated, but this depends on the plants and length of neglect. Very old blackcurrant bushes, for example, are best dug up and discarded. If the neglect has been for only a few years, however, renovation is possible (see opposite). Apple and pear trees that are past renovation can have their branches cut back and be crown grafted – but this is radical treatment and the tree will not bear fruits for several years.

FRUIT VARIETY CHECK

Where you are taking over a garden which has been part of an old orchard, if possible check the names of the varieties before grubbing them out. It may be that the variety is an old one renowned for its superbly flavoured fruits. Many apples now grown commercially are selected for their cropping, travelling and ripening value, rather than their flavour, and it would be a great loss if a good variety was grubbed out. Contact a local orchard or a horticultural society and take along a few fruits for identification.

If the tree is worth keeping, prune it in winter and spray with a winter-wash to kill insects and to remove lichens that so often accumulate on old trees.

A neglected garden may look fine at first, but plants may be smothering each other.

Throughout this book, advice is given about renovating specific plants, from shrubs and trees to climbers and hedges.

Fruit tree warnings

Before grubbing out an apple or pear tree, check that it is not a major pollen provider for the remaining trees.

Apart from branch and twig congestion, you may have to contend with a tree riddled with pests and diseases. Be prepared for regular spraying.

DON'T DISTURB!

If you have a tree that is past renovation and is to be cut down, first check that birds are not nesting in it. In many countries, it is illegal to disturb a nest with eggs or young birds in it.

Ornamental trees

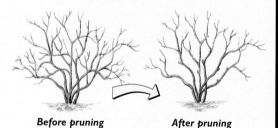

Before pruning   *After pruning*

Because ornamental trees need little regular pruning, even after several years of neglect they are usually easy to renovate. Often, thin shoots (known as water-shoots) grow from the trunk and lower branches, especially on neglected lilacs. Use a Grecian saw to remove them and, if necessary, a sharp knife to ensure the cuts are flush with the trunk. Some trees when neglected, such as the deep purple-leaved *Prunus cerasifera* 'Pissardii', also produce masses of thin, somewhat twiggy stems. Again, use a saw to remove them close to the trunk or branches. Take care not to leave unsightly snags.

When a large branch needs to be removed, cut it off in short sections (see opposite page).

Fruit trees

Before pruning   *After pruning*

Neglected apple and pear trees have masses of crossing branches and undersized fruits. Also, the tree is probably riddled with pests and diseases. Cut out cankered branches. There is then a judgement to make as to whether the amount of the tree that remains is worth saving; remember that renovation will take several years.

If the tree is worth keeping, during the first dormant season cut out all dead and diseased wood, as well as congested branches and shoots at the tree's centre. During the following year, cut back any excessively old branches, and in the following dormant season start pruning the smaller shoots. Spray the tree regularly and feed the soil around its base.

Fruit bushes

These are shorter-lived than fruit trees and therefore decisions about their removal are easier. If a bush cannot be renovated and restored to bearing fruits within two years, it is better to dig it up and plant a young, healthy bush. Blackcurrants can be completely cut down to soil level; it will be a year or so later that they bear fruits.

Both red- and whitecurrants grow on a short 'leg', 15–20 cm (6–8 in) long, and renovation will take slightly longer. During the first year, cut out dead, crossing and old wood. In the second year, attempt to rebuild a spur system that will bear fruits.

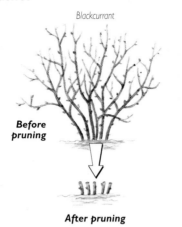

Blackcurrant

Before pruning

After pruning

Fruit canes

Cane fruits that have become formed of masses of tangled, old stems can be cut right down to ground level in late winter. Summer-fruiting raspberries and hybrid berries will bear fruits about 18 months later, on two-year-old canes. However, autumn-fruiting raspberries will bear fruits later the same summer, on one-year-old canes.

For all cane fruit regeneration, feed the plants in spring and regularly water the soil.

Before pruning

After pruning

Rose bushes

Before pruning

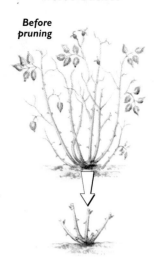

After pruning

If neglected, Hybrid Tea and Floribunda roses become overgrown with suckers and congested, old wood. Each sucker is best removed by tracing the stem back to the roots and pulling it off. Do not cut it off. Rejuvenation basically involves encouraging the development of young, new shoots from the plant's base. If badly neglected, cut out half of the old and thick stems to their base during spring; in the following year, cut out the rest. During each of these two years, cut out the stems evenly from around the plant, not just from one side.

CUTTING OFF LARGE BRANCHES

It is essential that large branches are cut off in small pieces, rather than all at once. If cut off in one piece, there is the risk of the trunk being damaged by the branch, when partly cut, falling and tearing the bark. Cut back the branch in several stages until about 45 cm (18 in) from the trunk.

1 *Use a sharp saw to cut the underside of the branch, half to two-thirds of the way through it.*

2 *From the top side, cut through the remaining part of the branch. Hold the branch.*

3 *To assist the cut surface to heal quickly, use a sharp knife to smooth the wound.*

4 *To prevent diseases entering the wound, paint the surface with a fungicidal paint.*

Equipment you will need

Strong secateurs that make clean cuts are essential for pruning shrubs, roses and thin stems on trees, fruit bushes and canes. For branches and thick stems, however, saws are essential. Long-handled secateurs, sometimes known as loppers, are ideal for cutting thick stems, especially those at the centre of a dense, prickly shrub. Hedges need sharp garden shears, or powered hedge-trimmers if the hedge is large. Always use powered tools with great care.

How much equipment will I need?

Safety with chainsaws

When cutting off a large branch or cutting down a tree, chainsaws are invaluable – but take extreme care when using them.

- *Keep children and domestic pets indoors.*
- *Do not use during wet weather.*
- *If electrical, use a power-breaker in the circuit to ensure safety if the cable is cut.*
- *Wear goggles, strong gloves and a jacket.*
- *Do not wear a scarf or necktie.*
- *Have an assistant with you.*
- *Do not stand on a box or ladder.*
- *Do not use above waist height.*

TOOLS AND EQUIPMENT

Secateurs *For general pruning*

These are available in two basic forms. The bypass type (also known as parrot or cross-over) has a scissor-like action and cuts when one blade passes the other. The anvil type has a sharp blade that cuts when in contact with a firm, metal surface known as an anvil. Both cut well, but must not be strained in cutting thick shoots.

Bypass secateurs

Anvil secateurs

RIGHT- OR LEFT-HANDED?

Most secateurs are for right-handed gardeners, but left-handed types are available and these make pruning an easier and more pleasant job for 'lefties'. These secateurs allow the cutting positions of the blades to be more easily seen, and therefore the risk of damage to buds is reduced.

Long-handle secateurs *For out-of-easy-reach shoots*

Also known as long-handled loppers, these have the same cutting actions as secateurs – bypass and anvil. Most of them have handles 38–45 cm (15–18 in) long and cut wood up to 3.5 cm (1½ in) thick. Heavy-duty types have handles 75 cm (2½ ft) long and cut wood 5 cm (2 in) thick. Additionally, some have a compound cutting action that enables thick branches to be cut with very little physical effort.

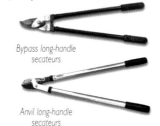

Bypass long-handle secateurs

Anvil long-handle secateurs

Garden shears and powered hedge-trimmers

Garden shears are ideal for trimming hedges and beds of heathers. Ensure that they open and close easily, cut cleanly and do not unnecessarily jolt hands and wrists. Where a hedge is large, powered trimmers make life easier. Most are driven by mains electricity, some by petrol-powered generators (ideal in areas far away from a power supply), while others are cordless and cut about 83 sq m (100 sq yds) between charges.

Cutting blades range from 33 to 75 cm (13–30 in) in length. Some have cutting knives on one side only; others have them on both sides.

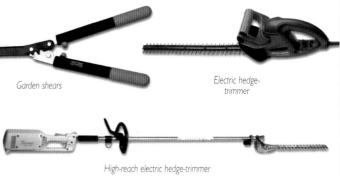

Garden shears

Electric hedge-trimmer

High-reach electric hedge-trimmer

TOOLS AND EQUIPMENT (CONTINUED)

Saws for all purposes *For cutting branches of all sizes*

Folding saws are usually 18 cm (7 in) long when folded and extend to 40 cm (16 in). They cut on both the push and pull strokes, severing wood 3.5 cm (1½ in) thick. Straight-bladed saws with fixed handles cut branches about 13 cm (5 in) thick, while Grecian types have curved and pointed blades and cut on the pull stroke. They are ideal for cutting branches in awkward positions. Bow saws are 60–90 cm (2–3 ft) long, with a blade kept under tension by a lever. They are ideal for cutting thick branches.

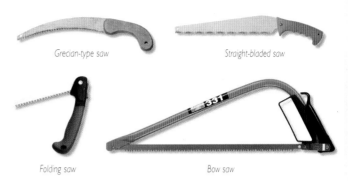

Grecian-type saw

Straight-bladed saw

Folding saw

Bow saw

Pruning knives
For experienced gardeners only

Knives have been used to prune plants for many decades, but their use is best reserved for gardeners with practical experience of them. They must be very sharp, and in the hands of a novice can be a lethal weapon. Therefore, they are best reserved for smoothing the surfaces and edges of large cuts on trees before an application of a wound paint. Take care when using a knife.

Pruning knife

High-reach pruners
For safety-first pruning

Also known as branch or tree loppers, these enable high branches to be pruned while the pruner stands safely on the ground. They cut shoots 2.5 cm (1 in) thick at heights up to 3 m (10 ft). They are ideal for pruning large and vigorous fruit trees.

High-reach pruners

Gloves and kneeling pads
When pruning roses

Stout but flexible gloves prevent hands being ripped by thorns, while a kneeling pad makes bush roses easier to reach. Kneelers are also useful as their side supports help infirm gardeners to get down and up easily without back strain.

Kneeling pad

Gloves

Knee pads

Buying good tools

It is false economy to buy a poor-quality gardening tool as it will soon fail and may harm you, especially if a powered type. In addition, sharp-edged tools may soon lose their sharpness. Therefore, always buy a reputable brand from an established store.

Hiring tools

Many gardening tools can be hired, but usually it is those that are only occasionally needed, such as chainsaws. Before hiring a chainsaw, confirm that it is in good condition, with a sharp chain and bottle of lubricating oil.

TOOL MAINTENANCE

Pruning tools must be kept sharp and in good condition if they are to operate and function easily and properly.

- Wash and wipe tools after use and coat bright surfaces with thin oil, especially if stored for several months.

- Chains on chainsaws need frequent checking during use, but first unplug the power cable.

- Check power cables at the end of each season and replace those that are damaged.

- Store equipment in an airy, waterproof shed. If it is slightly damp, wrap small tools in a dry cloth and place in a polythene bag.

GETTING A GRIP

Before buying a gardening tool, always handle it to ensure that it feels right for you. Pruning tools – especially secateurs – should be comfortable to hold and easy to use. If too large for your hand, it is difficult to put the desired pressure on the handles. If too small, there is a chance of fingers being pinched when handles are closed.

Check loppers to ensure that the handles, as the blades close and cut, do not nip and trap large hands.

When testing garden shears, check that as they cut they do not jolt your hands and wrists; some shears have rubber stops to prevent this happening. Additionally, check that the shears cut along their entire cutting edges.

Preparing plants for planting

What is pre-planting pruning?

This involves pruning both roots and shoots. If a bare-rooted rose, shrub or tree has long or damaged roots, they need to be shortened or cut out completely before planting proceeds. Additionally, damaged or misplaced branches and shoots need cutting out to create a balanced 'head'; a tree with too many branches on one side will look strange, as well as being more susceptible to damage from strong and gusting winds.

When planting, check that the top of the soil ball of a container-grown plant is slightly lower than the surrounding soil.

TRIMMING THE ROOTS

Preparing the roots is important for both bare-rooted and container-grown plants. Those of bare-rooted plants can be readily seen, and damaged or extra long ones identified. Use sharp secateurs to cut those of roses to about 30 cm (12 in) long. If left, they prevent the plant being positioned over a mound of soil in the hole's base and the roots evenly covered with friable soil. Damaged roots will not recover and may cause others to deteriorate and die.

The roots of container-grown roses and fruit trees also need attention. Trees left too long in a container before being sold may have contorted roots which will never properly anchor the plant. The container needs to be full of young, healthy roots that will quickly grow into surrounding soil when planted.

Getting plants established

Pruning roots and stems is not the only part of getting plants established. Erect 'guards' against rabbits if they are a pest in your area.

• Where a plant has been planted in early winter, in spring use the heel of your shoe or boot to refirm the soil. Frost tends to lift the soil, while strong winds may rock insecure plants and loosen their roots.

• Before refirming soil around trees that have been secured to a stake, loosen the ties. This is because the main stem will be slightly pressed downwards during firming and thereby strangled if the ties were not loosened. Firm the soil and then reposition and tighten the ties.

ROSE BUSH PREPARATION

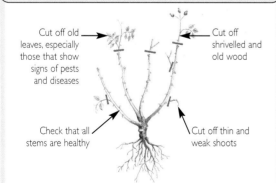

Cut off old leaves, especially those that show signs of pests and diseases

Cut off shrivelled and old wood

Check that all stems are healthy

Cut off thin and weak shoots

Checking roots: Cut back long and thin roots so that they will not impede planting. Cut out roots which may have been damaged when the plant was dug up from the soil. Also cut out roots damaged by pests or diseases.
Checking shoots: Cut out thin or decayed shoots, as well as leaves which may still be present.

FRUIT TREE PREPARATION

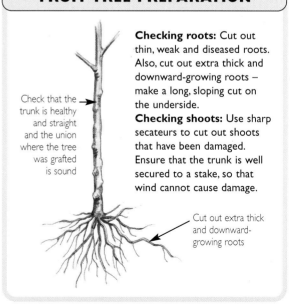

Checking roots: Cut out thin, weak and diseased roots. Also, cut out extra thick and downward-growing roots – make a long, sloping cut on the underside.
Checking shoots: Use sharp secateurs to cut out shoots that have been damaged. Ensure that the trunk is well secured to a stake, so that wind cannot cause damage.

Check that the trunk is healthy and straight and the union where the tree was grafted is sound

Cut out extra thick and downward-growing roots

Making the right cut

It is essential to prune just above a bud, rather than below it. By cutting slightly above a bud – without causing damage to it – it can be encouraged to develop into a strong, healthy shoot. If the cut is below, it will leave a long piece of stem above the bud positioned below it and this may cause the stem to die back and infect the entire plant. Additionally, long snags of dead shoots on shrubs and trees look unsightly and distract attention from the beauty of the plant.

Should I cut above or below a bud?

SHARP SECATEURS

If blunt secateurs are used, they often tear and rip the stem, making the correct positioning of a cut impossible. Secateurs that cause this problem have usually been used to cut shoots that were too thick for them. Bypass secateurs (also known as parrot or cross-over types) are more likely than anvil types to be damaged by cutting too thick wood. Under these conditions the blades tend to bend apart. However, anvil types when cutting too thick wood can cause bruising. Therefore, if sharp – and not used on thick wood – the bypass type leaves a more clinical cut that will heal quickly. Small secateur-like scissors are sold for severing herbaceous stems when cutting flowers for decoration indoors; avoid using these on woody plants as they will be strained and the stems damaged.

MIND THOSE BUDS!

When pruning, take care not to knock off or damage buds on shoots that have just been pruned. If this happens, it is necessary to cut to a lower bud (if that is in the right position).

Remember ...

- Before pruning a plant, thoroughly understand its nature so that it is correctly pruned.

- When pruning peaches and nectarines remember that there are three types of buds – fruit, growth and triple buds (for a detailed explanation, see pages 68–69).

- When pruning apples and pears, remember that some varieties bear fruits on spurs and others bear them at the tips of shoots (see pages 62–65).

CUTS FOR ROSES

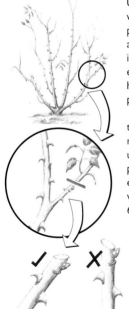

Until experienced, a few cuts will be made in the wrong place, either too high above a bud or too low and leaving it perilously balanced on the end of a shoot. If this happens, correct the problem as soon as possible.

Below are examples of the positions of cuts in relation to a bud, as well as using blunt secateurs. The position of the cut on the extreme left is the ideal, where a sloping cut is about 6 mm (¼ in) above a bud.

✔ Correct position; 6 mm (¼ in) above a bud

✘ Wrong angle; bud will be damaged

✘ Too close; bud will be damaged

✘ Too high; encourages decay

CUTS FOR FRUIT TREES

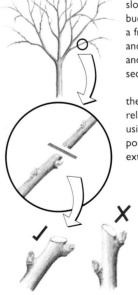

In the same way as for roses, the perfect cut has a slight slope and is just above a bud. The texture of wood on a fruit tree is usually denser and harder than on a rose and it is essential that secateurs are sharp.

Below are examples of the positions of cuts in relation to a bud, as well as using blunt secateurs. The position of the cut on the extreme left is the ideal.

✔ Correct position and angle

✘ Wrong angle; bud will be damaged

✘ Too close; bud will be damaged

✘ Too high; encourages decay

Philosophy of pruning shrubs

Do shrubs need regular pruning?

For many flowering shrubs, yearly pruning is essential to encourage the regular development of flowers. There are some that need only the occasional cutting-out of dead, aged and crossing stems, but for others the removal of flowered stems encourages the further development of flowering shoots. A few shrubs need just the removal of dead flowerheads. If pruning is neglected, a shrub's ability to produce attractive flowers is diminished.

PRUNING SHRUBS: THE GENERAL IDEA

For many shrubs, the purpose of pruning is to remove old, dead and crossing shoots, as well as those that produced flowers. This encourages the development of fresh shoots.

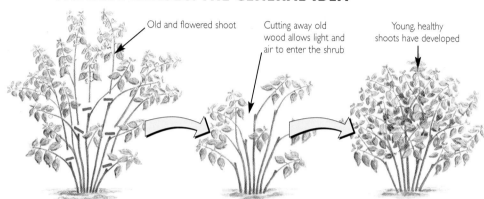

Old and flowered shoot

Cutting away old wood allows light and air to enter the shrub

Young, healthy shoots have developed

PRUNING EVERGREEN SHRUBS

These are clothed in leaves throughout the year, with new ones being formed and old ones falling off. Do not prune evergreens in winter; mid- or late spring is the best time, just when growth is beginning. However, if the plant is flowering, defer pruning until the blooms fade. The usual reasons for pruning evergreen shrubs are to create shapely plants and to prevent them crowding out their neighbours.

Examples of evergreen shrubs include *Berberis darwinii*, *Viburnum tinus*, Hollies, *Olearia* x *haastii*, *Choisya ternata*, Phillyreas and most Escallonias.

EVERGREENS FOR FLOWER ARRANGEMENTS

Many evergreen shrubs are in demand by flower arrangers, especially during winter when there is a shortage of other plants. When cutting foliage, always take shoots from the back of the plant and select them from several different positions. Use secateurs to cut stems just above a leaf-joint.

EARLY-FLOWERING SHRUBS

Early-flowering deciduous shrubs — flowering from spring to mid-summer — are pruned as soon as their flowers fade. This gives a shrub a long period during the rest of summer and into early autumn in which to produce fresh shoots that will ripen and be frost-hardy by winter. From spring to mid-summer of the following year these shrubs bear flowers on new stems.

Examples of early-flowering deciduous shrubs include Deutzias, *Philadelphus*, *Ribes* (Flowering Currants), Weigelas and *Syringa* (Lilacs).

Details of pruning these shrubs are given on pages 20–39.

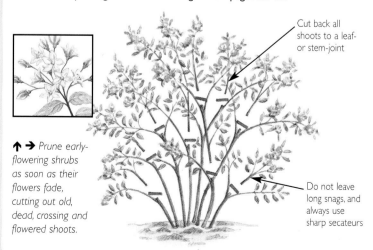

Cut back all shoots to a leaf- or stem-joint

↑ → *Prune early-flowering shrubs as soon as their flowers fade, cutting out old, dead, crossing and flowered shoots.*

Do not leave long snags, and always use sharp secateurs

LATE SUMMER-FLOWERING SHRUBS

Late summer-flowering deciduous shrubs are pruned during the following late spring. This encourages the development of shoots that will bear flowers later in the same year. If these shrubs were pruned as soon as their flowers faded in late summer or early autumn, any shoots that developed from the cuts could be damaged or killed by cold winter weather.

Examples of late summer-flowering deciduous shrubs include the popular *Buddleja davidii* (still often known as *Buddleia davidii*; Butterfly Bush), *Ceanothus* 'Gloire de Versailles' and *Tamarix pentandra* (Tamarisk). Incidentally, do not confuse this Tamarisk with the related *Tamarix tetrandra*, which flowers in spring and should be pruned as soon as the flowers have faded.

Details of pruning late summer-flowering deciduous shrubs are given on pages 20–39.

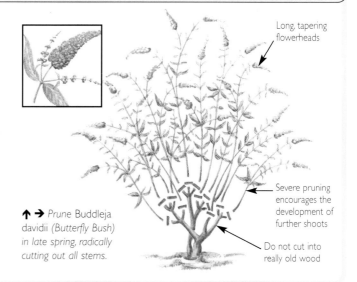

Long, tapering flowerheads

Severe pruning encourages the development of further shoots

Do not cut into really old wood

↑ → *Prune Buddleja davidii (Butterfly Bush) in late spring, radically cutting out all stems.*

WINTER-FLOWERING SHRUBS

Winter-flowering deciduous shrubs need little pruning. When young, prune them to shape to create an attractive outline. Later in their lives – as soon as their display is over, usually by early spring – cut out congested stems and those that have become diseased or damaged by severe weather. If left, they encourage decay to infect and damage other parts of the shrub. Keep the shrub's centre open so that light and air can enter. Incidentally, it is easier to control the size of winter-flowering shrubs than any other type.

Examples of winter-flowering deciduous shrubs include *Hamamelis mollis*, *Cornus mas* and *Viburnum* x *bodnantense*.

Details of pruning winter-flowering shrubs are given on pages 20–39.

STOOLING A DOGWOOD

Several Dogwoods are grown for their coloured stems, which are especially welcome in winter when they are free from leaves and low light can glance off them. Unless these plants are 'stooled' in spring by cutting them right down to within 7.5 cm (3 in) of the ground, they will not produce their annual display. Shrubs to look for with attractive coloured stems include *Cornus alba* 'Elegantissima' (red stems), *C. alba* 'Sibirica' (bright crimson stems), *C. alba* 'Kesselringii' (purplish-black stems) and *Cornus sericea* 'Flaviramea' (bright greenish-yellow stems); also known as *Cornus stolonifera* 'Flaviramea'.

Dealing with reversion

Occasionally, some variegated plants have stems that revert to an all-green nature. Usually, these are more vigorous than the variegated form and both look different from the rest of the shrub and stand above the normal level of the foliage. As soon as they are seen, cut back these stems to the variegated leaves.

Cut out completely any shoots with all-green leaves

Reversion can often be seen on plants such as *Euonymus fortunei* 'Emerald 'n' Gold', *Euonymus fortunei* 'Emerald Gaiety' and variegated forms of *Elaeagnus*, such as *Elaeagnus pungens* 'Maculata'.

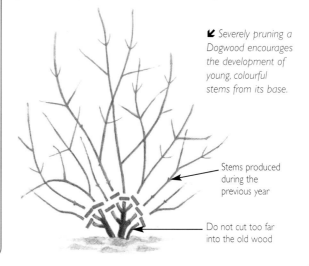

↙ *Severely pruning a Dogwood encourages the development of young, colourful stems from its base.*

Stems produced during the previous year

Do not cut too far into the old wood

Philosophy of pruning trees

Do trees need regular pruning?

Most trees need little pruning once they have been planted, securely supported and initially shaped. Those with an upright or spreading nature need careful initial pruning and training to ensure that the desired shape is achieved. Some trees have to be pollarded, and this is a salutary warning about planting trees in the wrong place. Trees are often best grown as specimens on a lawn or as attractive and dominant focal points towards the end of a garden.

The spreading and weeping Prunus x subhirtella *'Pendula' creates a glorious display in springtime, especially when it is underplanted with large, bright yellow, trumpet-type daffodils.*

REMAINING GOOD NEIGHBOURS

We all need good neighbours, but it is surprising how easily a tree with spreading branches that trespass on a neighbouring garden can cause trouble. Neighbours are entitled to cut off all branches overhanging their property, but these must be returned to you. They are also entitled to cut off roots that wander into their land. Some Bamboos have roots that travel long distances underground, occasionally sending up shoots that can damage patios as well as soft-skinned swimming pools.

Tall conifers are often a source of complaint, and the clear answer in a small garden is not to plant them – especially x *Cupressocyparis leylandii* which can grow to 15 m (50 ft) or more in 15 years and soon dominate a garden.

SELECTING AN ORNAMENTAL TREE

- Avoid Laburnums, as the bean-like seed pods when green and succulent are poisonous to humans and fish.

- Some trees, such as *Tilia* (Limes), encourage greenfly and exudations of sticky honeydew.

- Do not plant trees with fruits near pavements; the fruits become squashed and create a slippery surface.

PRUNING OBSCURITIES

We often consider the removal of branches and shoots to be the only way to prune trees and shrubs, but this is not so.

- Root-pruning was earlier widely used to reduce the growth of apple trees before dwarfing rootstocks were introduced.
- Bark-ringing was also used to reduce the vigour of apple trees.
- Thrashing mango trees was widely employed in India to encourage fruiting. Bamboo canes were used to severely thrash trees, knocking off leaves.
- Smoke was regarded in some countries as a remedy for barrenness. Wood and other rubbish was burned under trees.
- Collar pruning – cutting down plants to just below soil level early in the rainy season – was used on Tea plants in India and Sri Lanka to encourage the development of fresh shoots and to rid them of pests.

Ladder safety

When standing on a ladder to cut off a branch, have a strong helper with you who can hold it firm. Also, take care that as the branch falls it does not twist and knock you off the ladder. Wide-based ladders give greater safety than narrow types.

PRUNING EVERGREEN TREES

Evergreen trees need little pruning, other than cutting out misplaced branches when young. It is essential to create a well-balanced tree, with branches all around. Conifers are usually trouble-free, but ensure there is only one leading shoot (for specific advice, see pages 44–45).

Conifers when young and not established – with a large area of foliage and roots not yet firmly anchored in the soil – are especially likely to be weighed down and distorted by heavy snowfalls. Brush or scrape off snow, push the conifer upright and use an oblique stake to support the trunk; cover and firm soil over the roots. In spring, refirm the soil and water the entire area. After about a year, remove the stake. In windswept areas, it may be necessary to leave a supporting post in place for a few years. Evergreen conifers are especially at risk in winter.

SPECIMEN TREES

Specimen trees are traditionally found on large estates, and might be an Oak or an Ash with a large girth and height. Several Cedars, with their distinctive and dignified layers of branches, are other possibilities. However, inherited specimen trees can be small and slow-growing, such as *Morus nigra* (Common or Black Mulberry).

If you have inherited an old tree, it will require regular attention, often from a professional tree surgeon. Periodic thinning may be necessary, as well as cutting off damaged branches. Sometimes decay can be found in the junctions of branches, and this needs to be removed and a filler applied; thought must be given, however, to enabling moisture to escape.

If you want to plant your own specimen tree, ensure that the area is sufficiently large to accommodate it during later years. Some specimen trees are not ruined by branches being removed, but *Cedrus deodara* (Deodar) and other weeping conifers will never return to their former glory.

TREES WITH A SPREADING NATURE

Many deciduous trees have an attractive, spreading nature. Several flowering cherry trees have this relaxed appearance, which gardeners often find appealing. With these trees, as well as those with a natural weeping nature, it is essential to cut out the leading shoot when the tree reaches the desired height. During the following year, cut out shoots that are growing upwards and might replace the main stem.

Eventually, the tree will have spreading branches; the lower ones may need removal when they become too low. Remember not to prune cherry trees while they are dormant, but to wait until spring when their sap is rising. Most other deciduous trees can be pruned during their dormant period.

Few trees have such memorable appeal as those with a spreading and weeping nature. Here is the way to encourage them to spread.

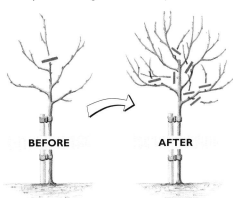

BEFORE   **AFTER**

TREES WITH A SINGLE STEM

Many deciduous trees – such as Birches and Poplars – have an upright nature, with a single, central stem that is able to continue growth upwards. Therefore, take care that the leading shoot is not damaged.

After planting, use proprietary ties securely (but not constrictively) to attach the main stem to a stout stake. During the following year, check that the ties are secure and cut off weak stems from the plant's base. In the following year, again support the trunk. During the subsequent year, and if the trunk is secure, remove the stake. Additionally, cut off a few weak branches from the tree's base.

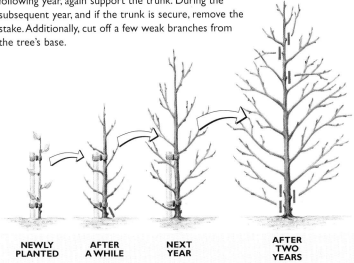

NEWLY PLANTED   **AFTER A WHILE**   **NEXT YEAR**   **AFTER TWO YEARS**

POLLARDING

Pollarded trees can be seen in many towns and cities, and invariably are the result of being too large for the areas in which they were planted. Pollarding involves cutting back main branches to the top of the trunk. It results in clusters of thin shoots growing from the trunk and abruptly cut-off branches. Because the area is constricted, either by houses or roads, pollarding has to be repeated every 3–4 years.

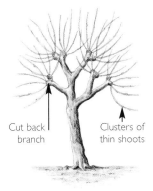

Cut back branch   Clusters of thin shoots

When a tree has to be pollarded, it is usually a sad admission that the tree is simply too large for its position.

Philosophy of pruning climbers

**Do climbers
need regular
pruning?**

Many climbers need little regular pruning. However, wall shrubs, such as *Jasminum nudiflorum* (Winter-flowering Jasmine), need more attention than evergreen Ivies which can overwhelm their positions. Many climbers are very vigorous and flood walls and trellises with flowers and leaves. *Fallopia baldschuanica* (Russian Vine), which eventually becomes invasive, reinforces the invaluable advice to match a climber's vigour to the available space.

PLANTING AND INITIALLY PRUNING A CLIMBER

Most climbers are planted as container-grown plants, at any time during the year whenever the weather allows and the soil is not frozen or waterlogged. However, spring is the best period, as climbers then have an entire summer in which to become established before the onset of cold, winter weather.

After planting, cut back stems by about one-third to a half to encourage the development of further stems at or near ground level, as well as to strengthen existing ones. Select 3–5 of the strongest stems and support or train them to reach a permanent supporting framework, such as a trellis. At the end of the growing season, cut these stems back by about a half. Additionally, you should drastically cut back any weak and ineffective stems.

If plants are not growing vigorously, repeat this pruning regime for a further year, until the climber has a strong framework of stems.

Pruning established climbers

The technique and timing for pruning established climbers and wall shrubs are described on pages 20–39.

• When pulling rough, sharp-edged or spine-clad stems from neglected climbers during renovative pruning, always wear a stout pair of gloves.

• Remove all prunings immediately after pruning is completed, rather than leaving them around a plant. Burn disease- or pest-infected stems.

Parthenocissus tricuspidata *(Boston Ivy) is a self-supporting climber that will soon cover a wall with its attractively shaped leaves. In autumn, the foliage assumes rich autumnal colours.*

SUPPORTING CLIMBERS

Climbers have varied styles of climbing; this indicates the type of support they need. Unless climbers are given suitable support, they will not be a success and will be difficult to prune (for pruning them, see pages 20–39).

Leaners ~ These need a framework against which they can lean and be tied. Plants that exhibit this nature include *Abutilon megapotamicum*, *Jasminum nudiflorum* (Winter-flowering Jasmine), *Solanum crispum* (Chilean Potato Tree) and climbing forms of roses.

Self-supporting ~ These climbers use aerial roots and adhesive suckers to scale walls and trees. They include *Campsis radicans* (Trumpet Vine), *Hedera* (Ivies), *Parthenocissus henryana* (Chinese Virginia Creeper) and *Parthenocissus quinquefolia* (True Virginia Creeper).

Tendrils or twisting leaf-stalks ~ These plants need twiggy hosts around which they can wrap their tendrils or leaf-stalks. They include Clematis, *Passiflora caerulea* (Passion Flower), *Tropaeolum peregrinum* (Canary Creeper), *Tropaeolum speciosum* (Flame Flower) and *Vitis coignetiae* (Japanese Crimson Glory Vine).

Twiners ~ These are friendly plants, and they gain support from twining around a neighbour. In a garden, they are usually trained to clamber over a framework of poles or wires. They include *Actinidia chinensis* (Chinese Gooseberry), *Actinidia kolomikta* (Kolomikta Vine), *Fallopia baldschuanica* (Russian Vine), *Humulus lupulus* 'Aureus' (Yellow-leaved Hop), *Jasminum officinale* (White Jasmine), *Lonicera* (Honeysuckle) and Wisterias.

PRUNING A WINTER-FLOWERING JASMINE

Jasminum nudiflorum flowers from early winter to mid-spring. It is not a true climber but a wall shrub, with flexible stems that need a trellis-like framework against which they can lean and be trained. Once established, it needs regular pruning, immediately after the flowers fade. To encourage regular flowering and to prevent plants becoming a mass of twiggy, congested shoots at their centres, it is essential that they are pruned every year.

1 *Use sharp secateurs to cut out crossing shoots, cutting just above a healthy bud.*

2 *To encourage the growth of fresh shoots, cut back sideshoots to healthy buds.*

3 *Cut out congested shoots from the centre of the plant to let in light and air.*

4 *Use soft string to tie shoots into place. Ensure that they are not constricted.*

RENOVATING A NEGLECTED CLIMBER

Many deciduous climbers if neglected become a mass of old, tangled, woody stems. The climber's base becomes bare and unsightly, with a poor display of flowers. Most climbers can be renovated by severe pruning, especially if in good general health. Climbers that are weak and with little new growth each year should first be fed and thoroughly watered for a season.

Renovation pruning is best spread over 2–3 years. At the same time, feed and regularly water the plant.

During the first year – and before cutting out a proportion of old stems – cut out dead and diseased shoots back to healthy buds. Then, cut out to near ground level a proportion of the old stems. Most neglected climbers can withstand having their stems cut close to ground level in spring. Use secateurs or long-handled loppers to cut down old stems. If there are some new stems, leave these in place. In one of the two following years, cut down the other old stems.

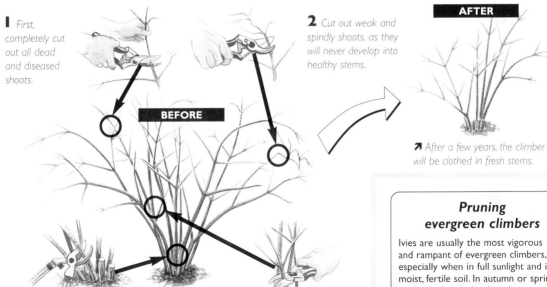

1 *First, completely cut out all dead and diseased shoots.*

2 *Cut out weak and spindly shoots, as they will never develop into healthy stems.*

BEFORE

AFTER

↗ *After a few years, the climber will be clothed in fresh stems.*

3 *Over two or three years, each spring cut out to near ground level a proportion of old stems.*

4 *If there are young stems, leave these in place, but remove congested, twiggy shoots.*

Pruning evergreen climbers

Ivies are usually the most vigorous and rampant of evergreen climbers, especially when in full sunlight and in moist, fertile soil. In autumn or spring, cut back shoots that have become invasive. Also cut out old shoots.

Be prepared for plants to be dirty and dusty; if necessary, wear protective goggles and a gauze breathing mask.

A–Z of pruning shrubs, trees and climbers

A practical guide to pruning specific shrubs, trees and climbers

Within this and the following pages is an instant yet authoritative guide to pruning trees and climbers, as well as shrubs grown in borders and against walls. They are arranged in alphabetical order under their botanical names. Common names are indicated, where applicable, as well as earlier and better-known botanical names. Pruning hedging plants is described on pages 40–43, and pruning conifers on pages 44–45.

Pruning hedging plants is described on pages 40–43, and pruning conifers on pages 44–45.

KEY TO SYMBOLS

Each plant's nature is indicated by the following symbols:

Tree

Shrub

Wall shrub

Climber

Bamboo

A | **A–Z OF PRUNING SHRUBS, TREES AND CLIMBERS** | **A**

Abelia x grandiflora

 No regular pruning is needed for this evergreen or semi-evergreen shrub, but cut out congested shoots in autumn to encourage the development of fresh growth. Cut out congested shoots on deciduous species in early or mid-spring to encourage the development of new shoots.

Abeliophyllum distichum

 Little pruning is needed, other than cutting out dead shoots in early spring or as soon as there is no risk of frost.

Abutilon megapotamicum

 In mid-spring, cut out straggly and frost-damaged shoots.

Abutilon vitifolium

 Prune in the same way as for *Abutilon megapotamicum*.

Acacia

Wattle

 These slightly tender evergreen shrubs and trees are best grown against a warm, sheltered wall. Once established and with a framework of branches, little pruning is needed. Large specimens can be cut back by two-thirds after the flowers fade. This will help to restrict their size – but do not do this too frequently, as each time the shrub will take longer to recover. Additionally, do not cut into really old wood.

Acer japonicum

Japanese Maple

 In late summer or early autumn, cut out straggly, congested and misplaced shoots. Usually, little pruning is needed; if cut back radically, their shape will be spoiled.

Acer japonicum

Acer palmatum

 Prune in the same way as for *Acer japonicum*. It is the small forms with coloured and dissected leaves that are mainly grown in gardens and these need only light pruning, other than shaping the tree when it is young.

Actinidia chinensis

Chinese Gooseberry / Kiwi Fruit

 No regular pruning is needed for ornamental specimens, but occasionally thin out and trim back long shoots in late winter.

Actinidia kolomikta

Kolomikta Vine

 Prune in the same way as for *Actinidia chinensis*. Usually it is left to cover a wall and only pruned when too large.

Aesculus

Horse Chestnut

 No regular pruning is needed.

Aesculus parviflora

Bottlebrush Buckeye

 Cut out old, congested stems from this suckering shrub at ground level in autumn. This encourages the development of fresh shoots. If this task is left until spring, there is a risk of the cut stems bleeding.

Akebia

 Little pruning is needed for this climbing, twining shrub, other than cutting out any dead and long shoots in spring.

Amelanchier lamarckii

Snowy Mespilus

 Little pruning is required, but thin out overcrowded shoots in early summer, after the flowers fade. *Amelanchier laevis* and *A. canadensis* are pruned in the same way.

Amelanchier lamarckii

Ampelopsis

 No regular pruning is needed, other than cutting out dead or overcrowded shoots in spring.

Andromeda polifolia

Bog Rosemary

Little pruning is needed, other than cutting out old and congested stems in early summer, as soon as the flowers fade.

Aralia elata

Japanese Angelica

No regular pruning is needed, although this shrub tends to spread and if this happens cut out shoots to ground level in spring.

Arbutus

 No regular pruning is required, other than cutting out misplaced and straggly shoots in spring. Additionally, where trees are grown for their attractive bark, cut out branches that obscure them.

Arctostaphylos uva-ursi

Red Bearberry

 No pruning is needed, as it dislikes being cut. However, in spring nip out the tips of young plants to encourage bushiness.

Aristolochia macrophylla

Dutchman's Pipe

Little pruning is usually needed, but where space is limited thin out shoots and shorten long shoots by about one-third in late winter or early spring.

Artemisia abrotanum

Lad's Love / Southernwood

 Cut out congested and frost-damaged shoots in spring, when risk of severe frost has passed.

Artemisia absinthium

Common Wormwood

 Annually, in mid- or late spring, cut back all stems to within 15 cm (6 in) of the soil.

Artemisia arborescens

Prune in the same way as for *Artemisia abrotanum*.

Aucuba japonica 'Variegata'

Spotted Laurel / Gold Dust

 No regular pruning is required. Occasionally, the edges of leaves are blackened and singed by frost. If this happens, cut back damaged stems in spring.

Aucuba japonica 'Variegata'

RENOVATION OF AUCUBA JAPONICA

Cut back any large, overgrown plants in spring to about 60 cm (2 ft) high. New stems usually develop from the shrub's base, although the plant may look unsightly until they appear.

Azalea

No regular pruning is needed. However, where bushes become congested, cut out a few stems as soon as the flowers fade.

Azalea

Azara

No regular pruning is needed. However, where shoots become damaged by frost, or bushes become 'leggy', cut stems hard back in late spring after the flowers fade.

Bamboo

This encompasses a wide group of plants. No regular pruning is needed, although where clumps become old and exhausted cut canes to ground level in late spring. Heavy snowfalls sometimes damage canes; badly damaged ones should be cut out at ground level.

Berberidopsis corallina

Coral Plant

Little pruning is needed for this slightly tender shrub, other than cutting out dead shoots in late winter or early spring. Additionally, cut out a few congested shoots so that light and air can enter the shrub.

Berberis

There are both evergreen and deciduous types, and little pruning is needed for either of them. However, where evergreen types become congested, prune them after their flowers fade; prune deciduous types in late winter or early spring (when the beauty of their berries is over). Cut old and exhausted shoots to ground level or to healthy main shoots.

Berberis

Betula

Birch

No regular pruning is needed, but where a branch is damaged or misplaced cut it out in late autumn. At that time there is less chance of the wood bleeding.

Buddleja alternifolia

As soon as the flowers fade in the latter part of early summer, cut back by two-thirds all stems that produced flowers. This deciduous shrub is sometimes grown as a standard tree, with a clear stem of 1.2–1.5 m (4–5 ft). This allows the branches to weep. Training is relatively simple: after planting, tie a single shoot to a stake. In the first year, allow the central stem to grow upwards, but remove all sideshoots. In the second year, cut off the top of the main stem when about 1.5 m (5 ft) high and allow stems close beneath it to develop into branches. When established, prune as for shrubs, but not so radically.

Buddleja davidii

Butterfly Bush

Annual pruning is essential – to encourage the development of young shoots that will bear flowers from mid-summer to autumn. In early spring, cut back all shoots to within 5–7.5 cm (2–3 in) of the old wood.

Buddleja davidii

Buddleja globosa

As soon as the flowers fade, usually by the early part of mid-summer, cut out dead flowers and 5–7.5 cm (2–3 in) of the old wood.

Bupleurum fruticosum

Thorough-wax

During late winter or early spring, cut back shoots fairly hard in order to encourage the production of fresh, young shoots.

Callicarpa

Beauty Berry

In late winter, cut out old and congested growths, retaining as much young wood as possible.

A–Z OF PRUNING SHRUBS, TREES AND CLIMBERS

Callistemon

Bottle Brush

 No regular pruning is needed, other than occasionally cutting out any misplaced stems in late winter.

Calluna vulgaris

Heather / Ling

 In early spring, use secateurs to cut back long shoots. Alternatively, use sharp garden shears to cut off dead flowers as soon as they fade.

Calycanthus

Allspice

 In spring, thin out congested bushes; retain as much of the young and healthy wood as possible.

Camellia

 No regular pruning is needed, but shorten long, straggly shoots in mid-spring in order to create shapely bushes.

RENOVATION OF CAMELLIAS

Camellias that are old and with bare stems and bases can be induced to produce further shoots by cutting them back by one-third to a half of their height in mid-spring.

Campsis radicans

Trumpet Vine

 After planting, cut back all shoots to about 15 cm (6 in) high. This encourages the development of shoots from around the plant's base. With established plants, cut back previous year's shoots to within 5–7.5 cm (2–3 in) of their bases in late winter or early spring.

Caragana arborescens

Siberian Pea Tree

 No regular pruning is needed. However, shorten long growths on young plants as soon as the flowers fade to create shapely bushes.

Carpenteria californica

  As soon as the flowers fade in mid- to late summer, shorten long, straggly and weak shoots.

Carpenteria californica

Carpinus

Hornbeam

 When grown as a tree, no pruning is needed.

Caryopteris x clandonensis

Bluebeard

 Cut back the flowering shoots of the previous year's growth in late winter or early spring. Cut weak shoots to near ground level, and stronger ones to healthy buds. This encourages the development of young shoots from ground level.

Cassinia

 In early spring, shorten the longest stems to keep these heather-like shrubs neat and shapely.

Castanea sativa

Sweet Chestnut / Spanish Chestnut

 No pruning is needed.

Catalpa bignonioides

Indian Bean Tree

 No pruning is needed.

Ceanothus

California Lilac

  Prune spring-flowering, evergreen, bush-grown *Ceanothus* after the flowers fade. To keep the shrub neat and shapely, shorten long shoots. Prune evergreen varieties growing against walls by cutting back strong sideshoots to 2.5–5 cm (1–2 in) of the main branches as soon as flowering ceases. Prune late summer- and autumn-flowering deciduous types in spring. Cut out thin shoots and prune stems that produced flowers during the previous year to 15–30 cm (6–12 in) of the old wood.

KEY TO SYMBOLS 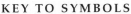 Tree Shrub Wall shrub Climber Bamboo

C | A–Z OF PRUNING SHRUBS, TREES AND CLIMBERS | C

Celastrus orbiculatus

Oriental Bittersweet / Staff Vine

 When allowed to grow freely over a tree, no pruning is needed. However, when grown against a wall or over a pergola, thin out unwanted or misplaced shoots in early spring. Also cut back main shoots by half their length.

Ceratostigma willmottianum

Shrubby Plumbago / Chinese Plumbago

 Shoots are often killed by frost and, if this occurs, in mid-spring cut the entire plant to ground level. This encourages the development of new shoots. In some areas, the shoots are not damaged by frost and in this case just cut out old, flowered stems.

Cercidiphyllum japonicum

Katsura Tree

 No pruning is needed.

Cercis siliquastrum

Judas Tree

No regular pruning is needed, other than shaping the plant when young. In later years, just remove dead shoots in spring.

Cestrum

Deciduous and evergreen shrubs or wall shrubs, some slightly tender and best grown in greenhouses. During late winter or early spring, thin out to their bases two- or three-year-old stems. Additionally, cut back lateral shoots to 15 cm (6 in) long.

Chaenomeles

Cydonia / Japanese Quince

Little pruning is required for bush-grown plants – just thin congested shoots after the flowers fade. When grown against a wall, cut back the secondary shoots at the end of mid-spring or into late spring.

Chaenomeles

Chimonanthus praecox

Winter Sweet

 Bushes growing in a border need little attention, other than thinning shoots in spring and cutting out dead wood. When planted to grow against a wall, cut out flowered shoots to within a couple of buds of their base after the flowers fade.

Chionanthus virginicus

Fringe Tree

 During mid-summer, after the flowers fade, thin crowded and congested bushes by cutting out spindly and weak shoots.

Choisya ternata

Mexican Orange Blossom

 No regular pruning is required, other than cutting out straggly shoots after the first flush of flowers has faded. Additionally, in spring cut out frost-damaged shoots.

> **RENOVATION OF CHOISYA TERNATA**
>
> *Choisya ternata* shrubs that are old and with bare stems can be rejuvenated by cutting all stems hard back in late spring. This will mean the loss of flowers for a year, but by the second year the shrub will be more attractive.

Cistus

Cistus

Rock Rose

Encourage bushiness by nipping out the growing tips from young shoots when plants are in their infancy. Later, plants do not like being pruned. Where plants have become bare and leggy, they are best dug up and replaced.

CLEMATIS
Large-flowered hybrids

These are popular forms of clematis, with large and dominant flowers. For pruning purposes, these hybrids were earlier divided into groups according to their parentage, such as Florida, Patens, Jackmanii, Viticella and Lanuginosa. However, such has been the hybridization of large-flowered clematis in recent years that as indicators of pruning techniques these divisions are now near worthless. Therefore, it is far better to be guided by the times at which they flower.

Clematis 'Nelly Moser'

Clematis jackmanii

Group 1 ~ Flowering initially from the latter part of late spring to mid-summer, they develop flowers mainly on short sideshoots on the previous season's growths. Sometimes, they develop further flowers at the tips of shoots produced the same year. During a climber's early years it is essential to encourage the development of shoots from the plant's base. Therefore, once established, and during its second year, in spring cut all stems to within 23 cm (9 in) of the ground. During subsequent years, as soon as buds start to swell in spring, cut out weak and dead shoots. Also, tie shoots to the supporting framework.

Group 2 ~ Flowering from mid-summer onwards, they develop flowers from the leaf-joints of shoots produced earlier in the same year. Prune them in spring, removing dead shoots and cutting out those that flowered during the previous year to a pair of plump, healthy buds.

Clematis alpina

A weak-growing deciduous climber but with a bushy nature that needs little pruning other than cutting out faded flowers. It seldom becomes too large, but, should this happen, cut back long shoots after the flowers fade, in late spring or early summer.

Clematis armandii

(including 'Apple Blossom' and 'Snowdrift') A vigorous evergreen climber that is best pruned as soon as the flowers fade, in late spring. Cut out all shoots that produced flowers.

Clematis chrysocoma

A deciduous climber, less vigorous than *Clematis montana* and therefore better suited to small or medium-sized gardens. It flowers mainly during early and mid-summer, and sometimes later. Therefore, cut back long shoots as soon as the flowers fade. This produces shoots for flowering during the following year. Sometimes it flowers on shoots produced early during the current year – this accounts for the later flowering. Where this climber is allowed to clamber into a tree, leave it unpruned.

Clematis flammula

A deciduous, bushy climber with flowers from late summer to mid-autumn. In late winter or early spring, cut back all shoots to strong buds at their base.

Clematis macropetala

Clematis macropetala

A slender, deciduous climber which flowers in late spring and early summer. As soon as the flowers fade, cut back the shoots that produced them.

As well as being grown against a wall or over a trellis, this clematis can be planted in a large barrel and its stems allowed to trail. When pruning, wait until the flowers fade, then cut back stems that produced them and trim younger stems to the base of the barrel.

KEY TO SYMBOLS Tree Shrub Wall shrub Climber Bamboo

Clematis montana

Mountain Clematis

 A vigorous, deciduous climber that benefits from yearly pruning. After the flowers fade, in early summer, cut back all shoots that produced flowers. This encourages the development of young shoots that will bear flowers during the following year. If allowed to clamber into a tree, leave it unpruned.

Clematis tangutica

 A deciduous climber with flowers from late summer to mid-autumn. In late winter or early spring, cut back all shoots to strong buds at their base.

Clerodendrum bungei

Glory Flower

 Little pruning is needed, other than cutting out the tips of frost-damaged shoots in spring. When shrubs become too large, cut them down to within 38 cm (15 in) of soil level in spring.

Clerodendrum trichotomum

Clerodendrum trichotomum

Glory Flower

 Prune as for *Clerodendrum bungei*.

Clethra alnifolia

Sweet Pepper Bush

No regular pruning is needed, other than cutting out any thin, weak and old shoots in late winter or early spring.

Clethra arborea

Lily-of-the-valley Tree

Prune as for *Clethra alnifolia*.

Colutea arborescens

Bladder Senna

In early spring, cut out weak, twiggy and thin shoots. Additionally, cut back strong shoots to within a few buds of the old wood.

Cornus

Dogwoods

 Tree forms need no regular pruning, other than occasionally cutting out a branch in late winter. However, those such as *Cornus alba* and *Cornus stolonifera* (also known as *Cornus sericea*) that are grown for their colourful stems need yearly pruning. In spring, cut all stems to within 7.5 cm (3 in) of their base. This encourages the development of fresh, young, colourful stems.

Corylopsis

Winter Hazel

 No regular pruning is needed, other than occasionally thinning out crowded shoots in late spring, after the flowers fade.

Corylus avellana 'Aurea'

Golden-leaved Filbert

 Yearly pruning is essential in order to encourage the development of fresh shoots and attractive leaves. In late winter or early spring, cut back vigorous shoots.

Corylus maxima 'Purpurea'

Purple-leaved Filbert

 Prune in the same way as for *Corylus avellana* 'Aurea'.

Cotinus coggygria

Smoke Tree / Venetian Sumach

 No regular pruning is needed, but as necessary shorten or cut out straggly shoots in early spring.

Cotoneaster

No regular pruning is needed, except to thin out congested shoots on deciduous types in late winter, and on evergreen types in mid- to late spring.

A–Z OF PRUNING SHRUBS, TREES AND CLIMBERS

Crataegus

Ornamental Thorn

 When grown as a tree, no regular pruning is needed.

Cytisus

Broom

 To encourage bushiness, trim off the leading shoots of young plants several times during their first summer. When established, prune plants that flower on the previous season's shoots as soon as the flowers fade. Cut all shoots back by two-thirds. For plants that flower on the current season's growth, prune in spring, cutting shoots hard back before growth commences.

Daboecia cantabrica

St Daboecia's Heath

 In late autumn, use garden shears to clip off dead flowers. In cold areas, leave pruning until spring.

Daphne

 No regular pruning is needed, other than cutting out dead and straggly shoots in spring.

Davidia involucrata

Pocket-handkerchief Tree / Dove Tree / Ghost Tree

 No regular pruning is needed.

Desfontainea spinosa

 No regular pruning is needed, other than occasionally cutting out shoots from plants that are too large for their positions, in late spring.

Desfontainea spinosa

Deutzia

Thin bushes in mid-summer, as soon as the flowers fade, by cutting out old, flowered stems to their bases or to soil level.

Dipelta floribunda

 In early or mid-summer, after the flowers fade, cut out a few of the old stems to ground level. This keeps bushes open and encourages the development of fresh shoots.

Dipelta floribunda

Eccremocarpus scaber

Chilean Glory Flower

 In late spring, cut out frost-damaged shoots. However, if the plant is severely damaged by frost, prune all stems to their bases in spring to encourage the development of fresh ones.

Elaeagnus

No regular pruning is needed, but cut out straggly and misplaced shoots in spring. Additionally, cut out all-green shoots from variegated species.

Elsholtzia stauntonii

Mint Shrub

Yearly, in late winter, cut back fairly hard the flowering shoots from the previous year. Also, cut out weak and twiggy shoots.

Embothrium coccineum

Chilean Fire Bush

 No regular pruning is needed, but cut out straggly growths after the flowers fade.

Embothrium coccineum

Enkianthus campanulatus

No regular pruning is needed, other than in late winter to maintain its shape.

KEY TO SYMBOLS Tree Shrub Wall shrub Climber Bamboo

Erica

Heath / Heather

 Tall, spring-flowering types do not need regular pruning, other than shortening long ends of straggly shoots in late spring, when the flowers fade. For lower-growing types, use garden shears in spring to clip off dead flowers from summer-flowering species. Clip winter- and spring-flowering types as soon as their flowers fade.

Escallonia

Bushes growing in borders need little pruning, other than occasionally cutting back shoots in spring or after the flowers fade.

Eucalyptus

Gum Trees

 Many *Eucalyptus* when grown as trees need no pruning, while others can be pruned annually, or periodically, to produce young stems and fresh leaves. For example, *Eucalyptus gunnii* when cut down annually in spring produces round, blue-green to silvery-white leaves which are often used in indoor flower arrangements.

Eucryphia

Eucryphia

No regular pruning is needed for established shrubs and trees. However, cut off the ends of shoots on young plants to encourage bushiness.

Euonymus

Prune evergreen species to shape in spring. Deciduous types need no regular pruning, but are improved by thinning out and shortening shoots during late winter.

Exochorda

Pearl Bush

 No regular pruning is required.

Fabiana imbricata

 Shorten long shoots after the flowers fade to encourage a bushy nature.

Fagus sylvatica

Common Beech

 No regular pruning is needed.

Fallopia baldschuanica

Russian Vine / Mile-a-minute Plant / Bukhara Fleece

Also known as *Polygonum baldschuanicum*. Pruning is not usually needed. However, when plants become too invasive, cut them back in spring.

Fatsia japonica

False Castor Oil Plant / Japanese Fatsia

 No regular pruning is needed. However, occasionally prune in spring to create a better-shaped plant.

Forsythia

Golden Bells

 Annual pruning is essential. In spring, after the flowers fade, cut out straggly and misplaced shoots. Additionally, shorten long and vigorous shoots.

Fothergilla

 No regular pruning is needed, other than occasionally to thin out overcrowded shoots in late spring or early summer, after the flowers fade. Additionally, cut out twiggy shoots.

Fraxinus

Ash

 No pruning is needed.

Fremontodendron californicum

Fremontia / Flannel Bush

 No regular pruning is needed, other than cutting off frost-damaged shoots in spring.

Fuchsia magellanica

Hardy Fuchsia

 Annually, in spring, cut back all shoots to ground level to encourage the development of fresh growth.

G — A–Z OF PRUNING SHRUBS, TREES AND CLIMBERS — H

Garrya elliptica

 Silk-tassel Bush

When grown as a bush in a border, it needs little pruning other than occasionally cutting out a few old, straggly or misplaced shoots in spring. When grown against a wall, cut back long, secondary shoots in spring, after the flowers fade.

Gaultheria mucronata

 Also known as *Pernettya mucronata*. This shrub requires no regular pruning. However, old plants often become leggy and benefit from being severely cut back in late winter or early spring. This encourages the development of new shoots from the plant's base.

Genista

Broom

 Once established, no regular pruning is needed. However, during infancy, nip out the tips of plants to encourage bushiness.

Gleditsia triacanthos

Honey Locust

 No pruning is needed, other than cutting out dead wood in early spring.

Griselinia littoralis

 Little pruning is needed, other than cutting out long and misplaced shoots in spring or late summer.

Halesia

Snowdrop Tree / Silver Bell Tree

 No regular pruning is needed. However, shorten long shoots as soon as the flowers fade, in late spring.

Halimium

No regular pruning is required, other than in spring cutting out dead shoots.

Halimodendron halodendron

Salt Tree

No regular pruning is needed, other than occasionally cutting out congested shoots after the flowers fade.

Hamamelis

 Witch Hazel

No regular pruning is required, but cut out diseased shoots as soon as the flowers fade. Additionally, remove straggly, crowded or crossing branches in late winter or spring.

Hamamelis

Hebe

No regular pruning is needed, but leggy shrubs can be severely pruned in mid-spring. Fresh shoots will develop from the shrub's base.

Hedera canariensis 'Gloire de Marengo'

Variegated Canary Island Ivy

Also known as *Hedera canariensis* 'Variegata'. This climber creates moderate growth during its first few years after being planted, but once established it becomes vigorous and can soon block gutters and penetrate cracks and crevices. Therefore, in late winter or early spring, check that shoots are not becoming invasive, and cut them back as necessary. Also cut back long stems in late summer.

Hedera colchica 'Dentata Variegata'

Variegated Persian Ivy

Also known as *Hedera colchica* 'Variegata'. Prune this vigorous climber in the same way as recommended for *Hedera canariensis* 'Gloire de Marengo'.

Hedera colchica 'Sulphur Heart'

Also known as *Hedera colchica* 'Paddy's Pride', this climber is even more vigorous than *Hedera colchica* 'Dentata Variegata' or *Hedera canariensis* 'Gloire de Marengo'. Prune it in the same way as recommended for *Hedera canariensis* 'Gloire de Marengo'.

Hedera helix 'Goldheart'

This small-leaved variegated Ivy is often allowed to climb a wall where, if it receives plenty of light, it often becomes invasive. Prune it in the same way as recommended for *Hedera canariensis* 'Gloire de Marengo'.

Hedysarum multijugum

 Thin out any old and weak stems and shorten straggly shoots from the previous year's growth in late winter.

Helianthemum nummularium

Rock Rose

 Shorten long and straggly shoots and cut off old flowerheads as soon as they fade.

Hibiscus syriacus

Shrubby Mallow / Shrubby Althaea

 Little pruning is needed, other than shortening long shoots in spring.

Hibiscus syriacus

Hippophae rhamnoides

Sea Buckthorn

 No regular pruning is needed, but, to ensure that the shrub develops a thick base, cut long and straggly shoots back to the old wood in late summer.

Hoheria

Lacebark

 In early or mid-spring, cut out frost-damaged and straggly shoots. At the same time, thin out congested shoots, especially on wall-trained plants.

Holodiscus discolor

Creambush / Ocean-spray

 No regular pruning is needed.

Humulus lupulus 'Aureus'

Yellow-leaved Hop / Golden-leaved Hop

This is a herbaceous climber and each autumn or early winter the leaves and stems die. Remove these in late autumn or early spring.

Hydrangea anomala petiolaris

Japanese Climbing Hydrangea

 Also known as *Hydrangea petiolaris*, no regular pruning is needed for this vigorous climber. However, cut out dead shoots in spring. Additionally, thin out congested and straggly shoots.

Hydrangea arborescens

Hills of Snow

Annually, in late winter or early spring, cut back all shoots that produced flowers during the previous year by about one-third to a half.

Hydrangea macrophylla

French Hydrangea / Mophead Hydrangea

There are two forms of this popular deciduous shrub – Hortensia and Lacecap. In late winter or early spring, cut out to their bases all shoots that produced flowers during the previous year. The old flowerheads are sometimes cut off in autumn, but in cold areas pruning is best left until spring – the dead flowerheads help to give the shrub protection against severe weather, as well as looking attractive when coated in frost.

Hydrangea macrophylla

Hydrangea paniculata

In late winter or early spring, cut back by a half all shoots that flowered during the previous year. If extra large flowerheads are desired, cut back the shoots more severely, by two-thirds.

Hypericum

St John's Wort

During late winter or early spring, shorten by about a quarter strong shoots that were produced during the previous season. *Hypericum calycinum* (Rose of Sharon) can be cut down to within 13–15 cm (5–6 in) of the soil every few years in early or mid-spring to keep it compact.

I   **K**

Ilex

Holly

No regular pruning is needed, other than occasionally to shape plants in spring. Cut back large or straggly shrubs in late spring.

Indigofera

Indigo Plant

 No regular pruning is needed, other than cutting out frost-damaged or excessively long shoots in early spring. *Indigofera heterantha* (also known as *Indigofera girardiana*) develops shoots from its base and if plants are excessively damaged by frost, or have become overgrown, they can be cut back severely in mid-spring.

Itea ilicifolia

No regular pruning is needed, except occasionally cutting out misplaced shoots in spring.

Itea virginica

Sweet-spire / Tassel-white / Virginia Willow

 No regular pruning is needed, except occasionally cutting out misplaced shoots in spring.

Jasminum nudiflorum

Winter-flowering Jasmine

 In mid-spring, after the flowers fade, cut out to within 5–7.5 cm (2–3 in) of their bases stems that produced flowers. Also, completely cut out weak and spindly shoots. For more detailed information on pruning this wall shrub, see page 19.

Jasminum officinale

Common White Jasmine

After the flowers fade, thin out the flowered shoots to their base. Do not just shorten them.

Jasminum polyanthum

Pink Jasmine

In temperate climates, this climber is usually grown indoors, but in mild areas it can be grown outdoors against a warm, wind-sheltered wall. No regular pruning is needed, other than occasionally thinning out overgrown plants after the flowers fade in early summer.

Juglans

Walnut

Walnut trees bleed when cut, so avoid pruning them. However, should it be necessary to cut out crossing branches or dead wood, tackle this in either mid-spring or late summer.

Kalmia

American Laurel

 No regular pruning is needed, other than removing dead clusters of flowers in order to prevent them forming seeds.

Kerria japonica

Jew's Mallow / Japanese Rose

 Annually, after the flowers fade in early summer, cut to ground level or strong growths all those shoots that produced flowers. For *Kerria japonica* 'Pleniflora' (Batchelor's Buttons), thin out shoots to their base to encourage the development of young shoots from the plant's base.

Koelreuteria paniculata

Golden Rain Tree / Pride of India

No pruning is needed.

Kolkwitzia amabilis

Beauty Bush

After flowers fade in early summer, completely cut out all flowered shoots to encourage the development of fresh, new growth.

Kolkwitzia amabilis

Laburnum

Golden Chain Tree / Golden Rain Tree

 No regular pruning is required.

Lapageria rosea

Chilean Bell Flower

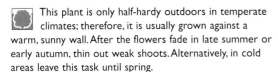 This plant is only half-hardy outdoors in temperate climates; therefore, it is usually grown against a warm, sunny wall. After the flowers fade in late summer or early autumn, thin out weak shoots. Alternatively, in cold areas leave this task until spring.

Laurus nobilis

Sweet Bay

Shrubs growing in borders need little pruning, other than occasionally cutting out a misplaced shoot in spring. However, shrubs grown in tubs and trained into desired shapes need pruning twice or more during each summer.

> **RENOVATION OF LAURUS NOBILIS**
>
> *Laurus nobilis* that have become overcrowded and rather unattractive can be pruned in mid-spring, severely cutting back into the old wood.

Lavandula angustifolia

English Lavender

Also known as *Lavandula officinalis* or *Lavandula spica*, this popular shrub needs annual pruning. In late summer, cut off old flowerheads and trim plants.

> **RENOVATION OF LAVANDULA ANGUSTIFOLIA**
>
> When plants become large and straggly, cut them back during mid- or late spring. This will encourage the development of shoots from the plant's base.

Lavandula stoechas

French Lavender

 Prune as for *Lavandula angustifolia*.

Ledum

 No regular pruning is needed.

Leiophyllum buxifolium

Sand Myrtle

 No regular pruning is needed.

Leycesteria formosa

Granny's Curls / Himalayan Honeysuckle

In spring, cut to ground level all shoots that produced flowers during the previous year. Sometimes it is necessary to thin out old shrubs, to enable light and air to reach the shoots.

Leycesteria formosa

Liquidambar styraciflua

Sweet Gum

 No regular pruning is needed, other than occasionally cutting out crossing and misplaced branches in early or late winter.

Liriodendron tulipifera

Tulip Tree

 No regular pruning is needed.

Lonicera japonica

Japanese Honeysuckle

 No regular pruning is needed, but occasionally thin out congested plants in late winter or early spring.

Lonicera japonica 'Aureoreticulata'

Variegated Japanese Honeysuckle

 No regular pruning is needed, but occasionally thin out congested plants in late winter or early spring.

Lonicera nitida

Chinese Honeysuckle / Shrubby Honeysuckle

 When grown in a border, this shrubby plant needs little pruning other than occasionally using secateurs to cut back large specimens in spring.

Lonicera nitida 'Baggesen's Gold'

 Prune in the same way as for *Lonicera nitida*.

Lonicera periclymenum 'Belgica'

Early Dutch Honeysuckle

 No regular pruning is needed, other than occasionally thinning out old and congested shoots after the flowers fade.

Lonicera periclymenum 'Serotina'

Late Dutch Honeysuckle

No regular pruning is needed, except occasionally cutting out old and congested shoots in spring.

RENOVATION OF HONEYSUCKLES

Honeysuckles such as *Lonicera japonica*, *Lonicera periclymenum* 'Belgica' and *Lonicera periclymenum* 'Serotina' eventually become bare around their bases with a tangled mass of old stems at head height, if pruning is neglected. If this happens, in spring cut the complete plant to within 38–50 cm (15–20 in) of the ground.

Lupinus arboreus

Tree Lupin

In late winter or early spring, cut out old stems. Also cut back strong growths to about a quarter of their length, and completely cut out thin, weak twigs.

Lupinus arboreus

Lycium barbarum

Duke of Argyll's Tea / Matrimony Vine

Occasionally, thin out shoots in summer after the flowers fade. Where shrubs have been neglected, cut them back in spring.

Magnolia

 Deciduous magnolias resent being cut, as large wounds do not readily heal. However, where the evergreen *Magnolia grandiflora* is growing against a wall, cut out outward-facing shoots in mid-spring.

Mahonia

No regular pruning is required. However, where *Magnolia aquifolium* (Oregon Grape) is being grown as ground cover, shorten long shoots in spring.

Malus

Crab Apple

 No regular pruning is needed, but cut out diseased, crossing or misplaced branches in late winter. Where fruits still persist on trees, leave this task until they fall. See pages 62–63 for pruning dessert and culinary apples.

Morus nigra

Black Mulberry

 Mulberries are likely to bleed when cut; therefore, only remove crossing branches and dead wood from trees when absolutely necessary.

Myrtus communis

Common Myrtle

Tender shrub often grown in greenhouses in cool areas, but in warmer and sheltered regions it survives outdoors. In spring, cut out to their bases long and straggly shoots. At the same time cut out frost-damaged shoots from outdoor plants.

Nandina domestica

Chinese Sacred Bamboo

Little pruning is needed, but thin out any dead wood and remove weak shoots as soon as the flowers fade.

Neillia

No regular pruning is needed, other than thinning out any congested shoots in summer when the flowers fade.

Nyssa sylvatica

Tupelo / Sour Gum / Pepperidge

 No pruning is required.

KEY TO SYMBOLS Tree Shrub Wall shrub Climber Bamboo

O A-Z OF PRUNING SHRUBS, TREES AND CLIMBERS **P**

Olearia x haastii

Daisy Bush

 No regular pruning is needed, other than cutting out dead shoots and shaping plants in late spring or early summer. Other Olearias can be treated in the same way.

Osmanthus

Devil-weed

 Little pruning is needed, other than trimming shrubs to shape in spring.

Paeonia suffruticosa

Tree Paeony

 It is slow-growing and little pruning is needed. However, in spring cut out dead shoots, and remove seed-pods as soon as the flowers fall.

Paeonia suffruticosa

Parrotia

 No regular pruning is required, but thin crowded branches in young trees in spring.

Parthenocissus henryana

Chinese Virginia Creeper

No regular pruning is needed. However, cut out congested or dead shoots in spring.

Parthenocissus quinquefolia

True Virginia Creeper

Prune in the same way as for *Parthenocissus henryana*, although it is a much more vigorous climber and, therefore, more thinning is needed.

Parthenocissus tricuspidata

Boston Ivy

 Prune in the same way as for *Parthenocissus quinquefolia*.

Passiflora caerulea

Common Passion Flower

In late winter or early spring, cut back old stems to ground level or to a main stem. Additionally, cut back lateral shoots to 15 cm (6 in) long.

Paulownia tomentosa

Princess Tree / Karri Tree

Usually, no pruning is needed. However, where it is grown as a dot plant, all stems must be cut down to soil level in early spring. This encourages the development of attractive leaves – but plants will not bear flowers.

Perovskia atriplicifolia

Russian Sage

Annually, in mid-spring, cut all shoots to about 30 cm (12 in) above the soil. This encourages the development of fresh shoots from ground level.

Philadelphus

Mock Orange

 As soon as flowers fade, in about mid-summer, sever all shoots that produced flowers. Leave young shoots, as these are the ones that will bear flowers during the following year.

Philesia magellanica

 Dwarf, suckering, slightly tender evergreen shrub. No regular pruning is needed. If it does exceed its allotted area, remove some sucker-like shoots for propagation before digging up and discarding them.

Phillyrea

No regular pruning is needed, other than cutting out any misplaced shoots in mid-spring. Where plants have been neglected, cut back old, congested shoots in late spring.

Photinia

No regular pruning is needed, but in early winter shorten long and straggly stems of deciduous species, and in mid- or late spring for evergreen types.

Pieris

Carefully cut off flowers as soon as they fade. Additionally, cut back long and straggly shoots.

P **A–Z OF PRUNING SHRUBS, TREES AND CLIMBERS** **P**

Piptanthus nepalensis

Evergreen Laburnum

 Also known as *Piptanthus laburnifolius*, this slightly tender, evergreen shrub needs no regular pruning; but cut out dead, old and worn-out shoots in late winter. At the same time, shorten long shoots by about a half.

Pittosporum

 No regular pruning is needed, but shorten long shoots in spring to keep bushes tidy.

Pittosporum

Platanus

Plane

 Cut out crowded stems and branches in winter.

Populus

Poplar

No pruning is needed.

Potentilla fruticosa

Shrubby Cinquefoil

Little pruning is needed, other than cutting out straggly, old and weak shoots at their bases after the flowers fade, in late summer and sometimes into early autumn. In cold areas, leave this task until early or mid-spring.

Potentilla fruticosa

PRUNUS

A wide group of ornamental shrubs and trees, as well as fruiting types that produce domestic fruits such as cherries, plums, peaches and nectarines (see pages 68–69). The pruning of ornamental types is described here.

Ornamental Almonds (deciduous) No regular pruning is needed, other than cutting back old, flowered shoots of *Prunus triloba* and *Prunus glandulosa* as soon as their flowers fade; prune them back to 2–3 buds of the previous season's wood.

Ornamental Cherries (deciduous) No regular pruning is needed, but when a large branch needs to be removed do this in late summer.

RENOVATION OF PRUNUS LAUROCERASUS

Prunus laurocerasus (Cherry Laurel) shrubs can be cut hard back into old wood during early or mid-spring in order to rejuvenate unsightly and neglected specimens.

Ornamental Peaches (deciduous) No regular pruning is required.

Ornamental Plums (deciduous) No regular pruning is needed.

Ornamental Cherry Laurels (evergreen) Cut back misplaced and large branches in late spring or early summer.

Pyracantha

Firethorn

 Shrubs grown in borders require little attention, other than cutting out misplaced shoots in late spring or early summer – but take care not to cut off flowers. For wall-grown specimens, shorten long sideshoots in mid-spring. However, do not remove too many shoots as, if left, they would produce flowers during the following year.

RENOVATION OF PYRACANTHAS

Pyracanthas grown against walls can be rejuvenated by cutting back all stems to old wood during spring. However, this will mean sacrificing flowers for a few seasons.

Pyrus salicifolia 'Pendula'

Weeping Willow-leaved Pear

 No regular pruning is needed, other than occasionally thinning out overcrowded branches in late summer. Also, shorten long, straggly growths.

KEY TO SYMBOLS Tree Shrub Wall shrub Climber Bamboo

Quercus

Oak

Cut out stems and branches in winter. Large, neglected, Oak trees usually need the service of tree surgeons, who have the right equipment to tackle large trees. For safety reasons, do not tackle large trees yourself.

Rhamnus

Buckthorn

In late spring, thin out old shoots on evergreen types to ensure that light and air is able to penetrate. Prune deciduous types in winter.

Rhododendron

No regular pruning is needed, but removing faded flowerheads by snapping them sideways helps to prevent the plant's energy going into the development of seeds rather than growth.

RENOVATION OF RHODODENDRONS

Many species and hybrid Rhododendrons that are aged, leggy and neglected respond well when cut back hard to old wood in mid-spring. However, do not prune grafted types or those with peeling bark – such as *Rhododendron barbatum* and *Rhododendron thomsonii* – in this way.

Rhus

Sumac / Sumach

 No pruning is usually needed, but if a mass of young foliage is desired cut all stems of *Rhus typhina*, *Rhus typhina* 'Dissecta' (also known as *Rhus typhina* 'Laciniata') and *Rhus glabra* to the ground each year between late winter and mid-spring. In cold areas, leave this pruning until late spring.

Ribes

Flowering Currant

Annually, in late spring, cut old shoots to ground level. This encourages the development of new growth from the base.

Robinia

False Acacia

 Regular pruning is not required.

Romneya

Matilija Poppy / Tree Poppy

Little pruning is needed for these sub-shrubby perennials, other than cutting out frost-damaged shoots in mid-spring.

Rosa

Roses are discussed on pages 50–61.

RENOVATION OF ROSES

Species roses need little pruning and the only treatment needed is to cut out weak, twiggy and congested shoots. However, neglected shrubs with bare stems can be cut down to within 30–60 cm (1–2 ft) of the ground in early spring. It means sacrificing flowers for a year or so, but will eventually produce a more attractive plant.

Rosmarinus officinalis

Rosemary

In spring, cut out dead shoots and shorten the tips of long and straggly growths. If plants become leggy, cut them back in mid-spring.

Rubus

Ornamental Brambles

Annually, in late spring, cut old stems to ground level on those species grown for their coloured stems. This encourages the development of young stems from the plant's base. For other types, cut to ground level a few of the old stems as soon as the flowers fade.

Ruscus aculeatus

Butcher's Broom

Little pruning is needed, except occasionally cutting out dead shoots in spring.

Ruscus aculeatus

A–Z OF PRUNING SHRUBS, TREES AND CLIMBERS

Salix

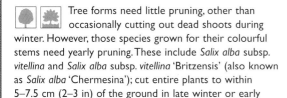 Tree forms need little pruning, other than occasionally cutting out dead shoots during winter. However, those species grown for their colourful stems need yearly pruning. These include *Salix alba* subsp. *vitellina* and *Salix alba* subsp. *vitellina* 'Britzensis' (also known as *Salix alba* 'Chermesina'); cut entire plants to within 5–7.5 cm (2–3 in) of the ground in late winter or early spring. This encourages the development of fresh shoots.

Sambucus

Elder

 Keep bushes neat and shapely by thinning shoots in mid-spring. Where forms such as *Sambucus racemosa* 'Plumosa Aurea' and *Sambucus nigra* 'Aurea' are grown for their attractive foliage, annually cut back all stems to ground level in late winter or early spring. However, in cold areas leave this job until late spring.

Santolina chamaecyparissus

Cotton Lavender

Use garden shears to lightly trim off flowers as soon as they fade.

Sarcococca

Sweet Box

 No regular pruning is needed, but where shrubs become congested cut out a few of the old stems to ground level after the flowers fade.

Schizophragma hydrangeoides

Japanese Hydrangea Vine

In autumn, cut out dead flowers and unwanted shoots from wall-trained plants. Those plants which are clambering into trees can be left unpruned and their shoots allowed to clamber and twine unhindered.

Schizophragma integrifolium

Prune in the same way as for *Schizophragma hydrangeoides*.

Skimmia

 No regular pruning is needed, but shorten long, straggly shoots in spring.

Skimmia

Solanum crispum

Chilean Potato Tree

 In mid-spring, trim back the previous season's growth to 15 cm (6 in) long. Additionally, cut out weak shoots and those that have been killed by frost.

Solanum jasminoides

Jasmine Nightshade

In spring, thin out weak shoots and cut out those that have been damaged by frost.

Sorbus

Mountain Ash

 No regular pruning is needed, but retain the tree's shape by thinning out shoots in late winter after the fruits fall. Additionally, where trees are grown surrounded by grass, remove lower limbs to enable easy mowing.

Spartium junceum

Spanish Broom

 Lightly prune young plants several times during their first year to encourage bushiness. When established, shorten stems by one-third to a half of their length in late winter or early spring. Trimming Spartiums in this way is claimed to encourage the development of early flowers.

Spartium junceum

KEY TO SYMBOLS Tree Shrub Wall shrub Climber Bamboo

S **T**

Spiraea 'Arguta'

Spiraea 'Arguta'

Bridal Wreath / Foam of May

 Also known as *Spiraea* x *arguta*, this popular shrub needs regular pruning. On both young and semi-mature plants, cut back flowering shoots as soon as the flowers fade, leaving 1–2 young shoots at the base of each shoot. Later, as the shrub develops, in late winter cut out as much of the old wood as possible, leaving the previous year's growth to produce flowers during the current year.

Spiraea japonica

 'Bumalda', and other forms of this popular shrub such as 'Anthony Waterer', should be pruned in late winter or early spring by cutting all stems to within 7.5–10 cm (3–4 in) of the ground.

Spiraea thunbergii

 Prune in the same way as for *Spiraea* 'Arguta'.

Spiraea x vanhouttei

 Prune in the same way as for *Spiraea* 'Arguta'.

Stachyurus

Little pruning is needed, but occasionally in mid-spring shorten long shoots to maintain the plant's shape.

Staphylea

Bladdernut

No regular pruning is needed, but occasionally cut back long shoots after the flowers fade in late spring.

Stephanandra

In late winter, cut out old and spindly shoots.

Stewartia (Stuartia)

  No pruning is needed.

Stranvaesia

  Little pruning is needed, but thin out crowded shoots in mid-spring. Also shorten long shoots.

Symphoricarpos

Snowberry

 During late winter, cut to ground level a few of the oldest stems. Also remove crowded shoots.

Symplocos paniculata

Sapphire Berry / Asiatic Sweetleaf

 No pruning is required.

Syringa

Lilac

  Yearly, after the flowers fade, use sharp secateurs to cut off faded flowers. Additionally, in winter cut out weak and crossing branches. In summer, cut off any sucker-like growths growing from the main stem.

> ### RENOVATION OF LILACS
>
> Lilacs that have been neglected and become unsightly can be made more attractive by cutting the entire plant to 60–90 cm (2–3 ft) above the ground in mid-spring. However, it then takes plants 2–3 years to produce any further flowers.

Tamarix

Tamarisk

 Prune the spring-flowering *Tamarix tetrandra* as soon as the flowers fade. Cut the previous season's growth back by a half to two-thirds. Prune the late summer-flowering *Tamarix ramosissima* (also known as *Tamarix pentandra*) in late winter or early spring, cutting back the previous season's shoots by a half to two-thirds.

Trachelospermum asiaticum

Where plants are becoming too large, in early or mid-spring thin out vigorous shoots.

T A–Z OF PRUNING SHRUBS, TREES AND CLIMBERS **Z**

Trachelospermum jasminoides

Star Jasmine / Confederate Jasmine

 Prune in the same way as for *Trachelospermum asiaticum*.

Ulex

Gorse

 No regular pruning is needed. However, where plants become tall and leggy, cut them back to within 15 cm (6 in) of the ground in early spring.

Ulex

Vaccinium

Blueberry

No regular pruning is needed. However, when deciduous types become overcrowded, they should be pruned during late winter by cutting old stems to soil level or to strong, young growths. Prune evergreen species to shape in mid- to late spring.

Viburnum

Viburnum

No regular pruning is needed for deciduous types, other than occasionally cutting out crowded branches after the flowers fade. Prune winter-flowering deciduous types in spring, and summer-flowering ones in mid-summer. Thin evergreen types in spring.

Vinca

Periwinkle

 When plants become excessively large, cut them back in early or mid-spring before growth begins.

Vitis coignetiae

Japanese Crimson Glory Vine

No regular pruning is needed. However, if plants become excessively large and rampant, cut out any old shoots during late summer. At the same time, shorten young shoots.

Weigela

Each year, after the flowers fade in mid-summer, cut down to soil level – or back to older wood – stems that produced flowers. This encourages the development of fresh shoots that will produce flowers during the following year.

Wisteria floribunda

Japanese Wisteria

Wisterias need regular pruning to keep their growth in check and to encourage the regular development of flowers. In late winter, cut back all shoots to within 2–3 buds of the point where they started to grow during the previous season. Where a plant becomes too large, also prune it in mid-summer; cut the current season's new shoots back to within 5–6 buds of its base.

Wisteria sinensis

Chinese Wisteria

Prune in the same way as for *Wisteria floribunda*.

Yucca

 No pruning is required.

Wisteria sinensis

KEY TO SYMBOLS Tree Shrub Wall shrub Climber Bamboo

Foliage hedges

What are the advantages of hedges?

Hedges are vital components of gardens, creating privacy from neighbours, dulling the raucous and often continuous note of road traffic, and helping to prevent animal access. Additionally, they have an aesthetic quality, with many revealing either beautiful flowers or colourful foliage that can create very attractive backgrounds. There are even some hedges, such as the **Dwarf Box** (*Buxus sempervirens* 'Suffruticosa'), that form essential parts of knot gardens.

INITIAL PRUNING

For all hedges it is essential to encourage bushiness, so that the base is packed with stems and leaves. Hedges which are not pruned when young invariably have bare and unsightly bases later in their lives. When planting is in late summer or early autumn, leave the initial pruning until spring of the following year. This is because young and tender new shoots that develop from late summer or autumn pruning may subsequently be damaged by winter frosts.

The initial pruning needed by hedges can be divided into three groups (see below).

1st YEAR

2nd YEAR

3rd YEAR

↗ To encourage bushiness in hedges in Group One (some are evergreen, others deciduous), initially prune severely.

↗ During the second year, prune less severely. Even so, this encourages the development of fresh, young branches.

↗ From year three onwards, less radical pruning is needed to ensure that the hedge is clothed in leaves.

Group One

Immediately after planting, cut back all shoots to 15 cm (6 in) above the soil.

- *Buxus sempervirens* (Box)
- *Crataegus monogyna* (Hawthorn)
- *Ligustrum ovalifolium* (Privet)
- *Lonicera nitida* (Chinese Honeysuckle)
- *Prunus spinosa* (Blackthorn)
- *Symphoricarpos albus* (Snowberry)

Group Two

Immediately after planting, cut back all leading shoots and long sideshoots by about one-third.

- *Carpinus betulus* (Hornbeam)
- *Corylus avellana* (Hazel)
- *Corylus maxima* 'Purpurea'
- *Fagus sylvatica* (Beech)

Group Three

Do not prune leading shoots, but cut back untidy laterals.

- *Aucuba japonica* (Laurel)
- *Chamaecyparis lawsoniana* (Lawson's Cypress) and its varieties
- x *Cupressocyparis leylandii* (but only for use in large gardens and as a windbreak)
- *Euonymus japonicus* (Spindle Tree)
- *Griselinia littoralis*
- *Hippophae rhamnoides* (Sea Buckthorn)
- *Ilex* x *altaclerensis*
- *Ilex aquifolium* (Common Holly)
- *Olearia* x *haastii* (New Zealand Daisy Bush)
- *Pittosporum tenuifolium*
- *Prunus laurocerasus* (Cherry Laurel)
- *Prunus lusitanica* (Portugal Laurel)
- *Taxus baccata* (Yew)
- *Thuja plicata*
- *Ulex europaeus* (Gorse)

RENOVATING NEGLECTED AUCUBA JAPONICA HEDGES

Large and overgrown hedges can be cut back to about 60 cm (2 ft) high in spring. Although the hedge will initially look unsightly, it will soon start to develop fresh, young shoots.

A–Z OF PRUNING ESTABLISHED EVERGREEN HEDGES

Aucuba japonica 'Variegata'
Spotted Laurel / Gold Dust
Pruning is not usually necessary for established hedges, but use secateurs to cut out old stems in spring, as well as those damaged by frost.

Berberis x stenophylla
Informal shrub with arching stems. No regular pruning is needed, but cut back large hedges after the flowers fade.

Buxus sempervirens 'Suffruticosa'
Edging Box
Use hedging shears to trim hedges in late summer or early autumn.

Euonymus japonicus
Slightly tender evergreen shrub with a dense, leafy nature. Use secateurs to clip the hedge to shape in mid-spring. For a more formal outline, use hedging shears to trim it during summer.

Griselinia littoralis
An attractively foliaged hedge for coastal areas. Use secateurs to trim back hedges in early or mid-summer.

Griselinia littoralis 'Dixon's Cream'
Prune in the same way as for *Griselinia littoralis*, but not quite so severely.

Ilex x altaclerensis
In mid-spring, use secateurs to trim back long shoots and to smarten up the hedge's shape.

Ilex aquifolium
Common Holly / English Holly
Prune in the same way as for *Ilex x altaclerensis*.

RENOVATING ILEX (HOLLY)
Where hedges have been neglected, they can be cut hard back in spring. Fresh shoots will develop from the hedge's base.

Ligustrum ovalifolium
Common Privet
Once this hedge is established, use garden shears to clip over it several times during summer.

Ligustrum ovalifolium 'Aureum'
Golden Privet
This plant is less vigorous than the all-green form and therefore needs slightly harder pruning during its early years. Once established, treat it in the same way as for *Ligustrum ovalifolium*.

Lonicera nitida
Chinese Honeysuckle
In the initial year after being planted, ensure that each plant is cut back by about a half, and in the following year cut back the young growth several times. During the following years, cut back all new growth by about a half.

Lonicera nitida 'Baggesen's Gold'
This is less vigorous than the all-green *Lonicera nitida* and therefore needs slightly harder pruning over the first few years.

Pittosporum tenuifolium
Use garden shears to trim established hedges in mid-spring and mid-summer.

Prunus laurocerasus
Cherry Laurel / Common Laurel
In late spring or late summer, use secateurs to trim back long shoots. Additionally, large hedges can be cut back hard in spring.

Prunus lusitanica
Portugal Laurel
Prune in the same way as for *Prunus laurocerasus*.

PRUNING ESTABLISHED DECIDUOUS HEDGES

Berberis thunbergii 'Atropurpurea Nana'
A dwarf Berberis with rich reddish-purple leaves. Use secateurs to trim to shape in winter.

Carpinus betulus
Common Hornbeam / European Hornbeam
Forms a large hedge. Use hedging shears to clip the plants during mid-summer. Trim young hedges lightly, but established ones more severely.

Fagus sylvatica
Common Beech
Once established, use garden shears or powered equipment to trim the hedge in mid- or late summer.

SHAPING THE TOPS OF HEDGES

Flat top

Rounded top

Pointed top

In regions where snowfalls are heavy, when clipping hedges, create either a rounded or a sloping top so that snow has the opportunity to fall off. If the top is flat, the hedge may become distorted under the weight of snow. In warm areas, where there is little risk of snow, hedges can be given a square, clinical outline. Where flat-topped hedges have been badly damaged by heavy snowfalls, with the sides splaying outwards, use strong wire to repair them. About 30 cm (1 ft) from the top, delve into the hedge and wire together some of the splayed stems.

Flowering hedges

When should I prune my flowering hedge?

Most hedges that flower in spring can be pruned as soon as the flowers fade in early summer. With hedges that flower in late summer or early autumn, leave pruning until the following spring. There are many superb flowering hedges – of all sizes – for gardens, and below is a comprehensive range of them. Some of these are large and dominant, while others, such as Lavender, are relatively small and ideal for forming hedges within a garden.

A–Z OF PRUNING FLOWERING HEDGES

Pruning flowering hedges is no more difficult than looking after a flowering shrub in a border. It is essential, however, to tackle the task at the right time. Here is the essential information you will need to prune them correctly.

Berberis darwinii
Darwin's Berberis
Pretty, evergreen shrub that forms an attractive hedge. After the flowers fade in early summer, use secateurs to cut back long stems to create a hedge with uniform thickness and shape.

Berberis x stenophylla
Prune this large, spreading, evergreen hybrid hedge plant in the same way as for *Berberis darwinii*.

Cotoneaster lacteus

Cotoneaster lacteus
A strongly growing evergreen shrub. As soon as the flowers fade, use secateurs to cut off long shoots. At the same time, cut back the current season's shoots to where the berries are forming.

Cotoneaster simonsii
A semi-evergreen shrub with an upright nature, often used to create an informal hedge. Use secateurs to prune hedges during late winter or early spring, cutting out long shoots.

Crataegus monogyna

Crataegus monogyna
Common Hawthorn / May / Quick
A hardy, deciduous tree that forms an attractive, countrified hedge. Use hedging shears to trim the hedge, at any time after the flowers fade and until late winter.

Escallonia
Once a hedge is established, cut the shoots hard back after the flowers fade. However, the hedge can be encouraged to produce more flowers by only lightly trimming the stems.

Fuchsia magellanica
Hardy Fuchsia
Often grown as an informal hedge in warm, sheltered, coastal areas. Annually, in spring, cut all stems to ground level. This encourages the development of young shoots.

Lavandula angustifolia

Lavandula angustifolia
English Lavender
Also known as *Lavandula spica* or *Lavandula officinalis*. Nip out the growing tips of plants soon after the hedge has been planted to encourage bushiness. Use garden shears to trim established hedges to shape in early or mid-spring. When hedges have become straggly, prune them more severely.

Olearia x haastii

Olearia x haastii
Daisy Bush
Use secateurs in mid-spring to cut out dead shoots; at the same time, cut back long shoots to create an informal outline to the hedge.

Potentilla fruticosa
Shrubby Cinquefoil
Use secateurs to cut off the tips of shoots as soon as the flowers fade. Additionally, cut out straggly shoots.

A–Z OF PRUNING FLOWERING HEDGES (CONTINUED)

Prunus x cistena

Prunus x cistena
Purple-leaf Sand Cherry
Once established, use secateurs to trim the hedge to shape after the flowers fade in late spring.

Pyracantha rogersiana

Pyracantha rogersiana
Firethorn
Immediately after planting, use secateurs to cut plants back by a half; during the following summer cut back young shoots by about 15 cm (6 in). Repeat this pruning of young shoots during the following year. When established, trim in early summer.

Rhododendron luteum
No regular pruning is needed, except cutting out crossing branches or dead shoots as soon as the flowers fade.

Rosmarinus officinalis

Rosmarinus officinalis
In early spring, use secateurs to cut out dead, misplaced and straggly shoots.

Symphoricarpos albus

Symphoricarpos albus 'White Hedge'
Snowberry
In winter, thin out overgrown hedges. Also, use secateurs to trim established hedges to shape in summer.

Tamarix ramosissima
Tamarisk
Also known as *Tamarix pentandra*. In mild, coastal areas, this is an ideal informal hedge. Early pruning is essential in order to create a hedge that has a bushy base.

Prune newly planted plants to 30 cm (12 in) high. Later, use secateurs to cut out the tips of sideshoots when they are 15 cm (6 in) long. Once the hedge is established, use secateurs in late winter or early spring to cut back the previous season's shoots to within 15 cm (6 in) of the points from where they originated.

Viburnum tinus
Laurustinus
No regular pruning is needed. However, after the flowers fade in spring, use secateurs to cut out dead and misplaced shoots.

This is a resilient shrub that invariably creates a superb display of flowers from early winter to mid-spring – and sometimes slightly later.

A–Z OF PRUNING CONIFEROUS HEDGES

Chamaecyparis lawsoniana
Lawson's Cypress
Popular hedging conifer, with many varieties. Once established, use hedging shears or powered clippers to trim hedges in early summer and early autumn. When attempting to limit the hedge's size, cut off the top 15–20 cm (6–8 in) below the desired height. New shoots will clothe the hedge's top.

x Cupressocyparis leylandii
Leyland Cypress
Unless the garden is extra large, never consider planting this rapid-growing conifer. It is best suited for forming a tall windbreak on a large estate. Use garden shears or powered shears to trim the hedge to shape in late summer and early autumn. When trying to limit the height of the hedge,

cut off the top about 30 cm (12 in) below the desired height. Shoots later grow and create an attractive top.

Cupressus macrocarpa 'Goldcrest'
Use garden shears or powered shears to trim this hedge during its early years. Afterwards, little trimming is needed, other than limiting its height. Cut off the top when 30 cm (12 in) below the desired height.

Taxus baccata
Common Yew / English Yew
It is best to plant small plants, and when they are 30 cm (12 in) tall nip out the growing points to encourage bushiness. Removing the growing points is essential during the first few years. Once the hedge is established, use garden shears or

powered clippers to trim plants during late summer.

> **WARNING**
> *Do not plant this hedge where cattle can reach the foliage, since it is poisonous.*

Thuja occidentalis
White Cedar
Use hedging shears or powered cutters to trim established hedges in late summer. When limiting its height, cut off the top 15–20 cm (6–8 in) below the desired height.

Thuja plicata
Western Red Cedar
Prune in the same way as for *Thuja occidentalis*.

Conifers

Does my specimen conifer need pruning?

Conifers never fail to create distinctive and dignified features in gardens. Several species are ideal for forming screens, while others produce eye-catching features in lawns or as focal points towards the end of a garden, either on their own or in groups. It is essential to check conifers during their infancy to ensure that there is just one leading shoot. If two are present, the conifer's shape may be spoiled, especially when seen from a distance.

A–Z OF PRUNING EVERGREEN CONIFERS

Most conifers are evergreen and create an impression of perpetual greenness. However, during each year new leaves appear and a few fall off. As conifers grow, some of the lower branches become bare of foliage and are unattractive. These should be cut off close to the trunk. This especially happens to conifers such as Chamaecyparis when grown close together. Here are the pruning techniques to use for some popular conifers.

Abies
Silver Fir
Little pruning is needed, other than checking trees while young. Where there are two leading shoots, in spring remove one of them. Additionally, cut out sideshoots that might later compete with the leading shoot.

Araucaria araucana

Araucaria araucana
Monkey Puzzle
No pruning is needed. Occasionally, the lower branches fall off – check that the trunk has not been damaged.

Calocedrus decurrens
Incense Cedar
Also known as *Libocedrus decurrens*. No regular pruning is needed, but check that there is only one leading shoot. Prune in spring.

Cedrus
Cedar
No regular pruning is needed, but during early years check that there is only one leading shoot. When large branches have to be cut off, do this in late winter or early spring.

Cryptomeria
Japanese Cedar
No regular pruning is needed, but ensure that plants do not have two leading shoots. Prune in spring.

x Cupressocyparis leylandii

x Cupressocyparis leylandii
Leyland Cypress
No regular pruning is needed, other than checking that plants do not have two leading shoots. Prune in spring.

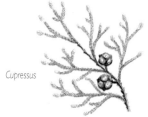
Cupressus

Cupressus
Cypress
No regular pruning is needed, other than ensuring there is only one leading shoot. Prune in spring.

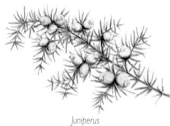
Juniperus

Juniperus
Juniper
No pruning is needed, but check that there is only one leading shoot. Where necessary, prune in spring.

Picea

Picea
Spruce
No regular pruning is needed, other than ensuring there is only one leading shoot; cut out the twin shoot as soon as it is noticed.

Pinus
Pine
No pruning is needed, except to ensure that there is only one leading shoot. If the leading shoot becomes damaged, remove all but the strongest from the growth immediately below. Do this as soon as possible after the problem is seen.

A-Z OF PRUNING EVERGREEN CONIFERS (CONTINUED)

Taxus
Yew

No regular pruning is needed. However, cut out clusters of sucker-like shoots that appear on the tree's trunk. This operation can be carried out at any time.

Thuja
Arborvitae

No regular pruning is needed, but ensure there is only one leading shoot. Cut out any others in spring.

Thujopsis dolabrata

Thujopsis dolabrata
Hiba Arborvitae / False Arborvitae

Bushy forms need no pruning, but where a specimen shows signs of forming a tree remove the lower branches in early or mid-spring.

Tsuga
Hemlock

No regular pruning is needed, other than to check that there is only one leading shoot. Prune in spring.

A-Z OF PRUNING DECIDUOUS CONIFERS

These are conifers that lose their foliage in autumn and produce fresh leaves in spring. There are fewer of them than the 'evergreen' types.

Ginkgo biloba
Maidenhair Tree

This distinctive conifer resents being pruned; cut shoots are likely to die back. It often has an irregular outline – this is part of the attractiveness of a superb conifer that seldom fails to gain attention.

Larix
Larch

No regular pruning is needed, but check that there is only one leading shoot. Cut out any other as soon as it is noticed.

Metasequoia glyptostroboides
Dawn Redwood

No regular pruning is needed, but check that there is only one leading shoot. Occasionally, the leading shoot is damaged by severe frost and if this happens cut back to a strong shoot lower down. Prune in mid-spring.

Taxodium distichum
Swamp Cypress / Bald Cypress

No regular pruning is needed, other than to check that there is only one leading shoot. Cut out any other as soon as it is seen. A symmetrical outline is part of the beauty of this distinctive conifer.

PRUNING PALMS

The most popular palm in temperate climates is *Trachycarpus fortunei* (Chusan Palm), which creates a semi-tropical feature in warm, sheltered gardens. It is also known as the Fan Palm, on account of its palm-like leaves, which are often more than 90 cm (3 ft) wide and grow on stems to 90 cm (3 ft) long. This palm does not need pruning, but remove damaged leaves, taking care not to disturb or spoil the coarse, stiff, dark fibres that clothe the trunk. These fibres are the disintegrated sheathing bases of the leaves.

Chamaerops humilis (Dwarf Fan Palm) is sometimes grown in warm and sheltered areas in temperate climates. However, it is better suited to the weather-comfort regions of the Mediterranean. Similarly to *Trachycarpus fortunei*, it does not need regular pruning, other than cutting off dead and damaged leaves.

STAKING CONIFERS

Eventually, conifers are self-supporting, but during their early years a strong, vertical stake ensures that growth is upright and that corrective pruning is not later needed. After preparing the planting position, knock into the ground a strong stake, so that its base is about 45 cm (18 in) in the soil and its top 60–75 m (2–2½ ft) above the soil, although this will be influenced by the height of the conifer. Position the conifer so that the stake is on the windward side, so that wind does not blow the trunk on to the stake and cause the two to rub against each other. Use proprietary tree-ties to secure the trunk to the stake.

Where an established conifer has blown over, use an oblique stake. Knock the stake into the soil so that its top is directed into the prevailing wind, and its top crosses the trunk. Secure the two with a tree-tie.

Oblique stakes are easy to install, but if the conifer is grown as a specimen on a lawn it is then difficult to cut grass close to the trunk.

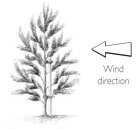

Wind direction

Use a vertical stake for a newly planted tree.

Wind direction

Oblique stakes are ideal for replacing broken stakes.

Forming arches and tunnels

How do I create a flowering arch?

Arches and tunnels create both eye-catching and practical features in gardens and many, once established, require little attention. Arches through hedges formed of the deciduous Beech or evergreen Yew create sudden entrances into other parts of a garden. Tunnels festooned with arch-trained flowering trees like Laburnum and climbers such as Wisteria reveal greater mystery and expectancy of what lies beyond the tunnel's end.

CHOOSING PLANTS

There are several choices of plants for clothing arches and tunnels, including Laburnum, which produces a profusion of yellow flowers in late spring and early summer. Flowering climbers and trained fruit trees can also work well in this situation. Climbing roses are another possibility, but it is important to ensure that thorns cannot come into contact with people, especially those who have limited vision. Constructing a continuous strip of paving slabs down the centre of the path, with gravel on either side, will give a sound warning if thorn-covered stems are too near.

CREATING LABURNUM TUNNELS

↑ *Laburnum flowers during late spring and early summer. Here, a small-leaved Box forms miniature hedges beneath the arches.*

Construct a metal or wood tunnel over a path. Ready-made tunnels are available, in widths ranging from 1.5 to 4.8 m (5–16 ft). The wider and higher ones are best suited for Laburnum, which has bunches of flowers that can hang for 30 cm (12 in). Ideally, choose a tunnel about 3.6 m (12 ft) wide and 2.4 m (8 ft) high. First, plant a *Laburnum* x *watereri* 'Vossii' 1.2 m (4 ft) in from each corner of the arch, with others spaced about 2.4 m (8 ft) apart. Initially, you should train the stems upright, at the same time taking lateral shoots along the supporting wires.

Laburnum responds well to spur pruning; in winter, prune shoots that are growing inwards or outwards from the arch, cutting them back to three buds. Cut back lateral shoots when they fill the allotted space, and tie in and train the main vertical shoots over the arch. Additionally, cut out damaged and weak shoots. When shoots are horizontal at the top of the arch, this especially encourages the development of flowers.

→ *Even during winter, when plants are bare of leaves, a Laburnum tunnel is attractive, with low rays from the sun highlighting the bark. Pruning is done during winter (see above right).*

WINTER　　　　**SUMMER**

← *In summer, the tunnel becomes flooded with pendulous clusters of yellow, slightly fragrant flowers. A Laburnum tunnel is an asset to any garden.*

CREATING PEAR AND APPLE TUNNELS

Metal arches for pear and apple tunnels do not need to be as large as those for Laburnum; those 1.8–2.4 m (6–8 ft) wide and 2.1–2.4 m (7–8 ft) high are better. Plant and prune the plants in exactly the same way as for espaliers (see pages 64–65). Carefully, but securely, tie the stems over the arch, taking care not to constrict them. Regularly check the ties as the stems thicken.

FRUIT ARCH

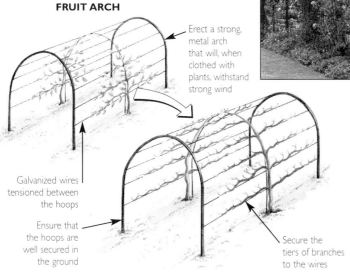

Erect a strong, metal arch that will, when clothed with plants, withstand strong wind

Galvanized wires tensioned between the hoops

Ensure that the hoops are well secured in the ground

Secure the tiers of branches to the wires

↑ *Fruit tunnels can create attractive flowering features during spring, as well as bearing fruits later in the year.*

← *If possible, orientate the tunnel north to south; this ensures that plants on both sides receive an equal amount of sunlight and therefore the plants develop evenly. The tunnel is a handsome feature and helps to separate one part of the garden from another.*

ARCHES IN HEDGES

→ *Arches with flattened tops initially need support from a framework of wood or wires. Wide arches are vulnerable to damage from heavy snowfalls.*

Flattened top, wide arch

→ *High-centred arches are dramatic and can introduce a Moorish feel to gardens. This one is formed from the slow-growing but densely foliaged Yew.*

High-centred arch

→ *Rounded arches that have a traditional English nature are easily created with Common Beech. This forms a strong arch that will withstand the rigours of winter.*

Rounded arch

Pleaching

The art of pleaching, where a hedge is created at head height, dates back several centuries. Lateral stems are trained to form an interlaced screen. Traditionally, Tilia x europaea (European Lime) was used, but it attracts greenfly and results in sticky honeydew falling to the ground. An alternative is Tilia x euchlora (Caucasian Lime). Hornbeam, Beech and Wisteria can also be trained in this way.

INITIAL PLANTING

Position individual trees in two distinct rows

CLIPPED PLANTS

Plant trees 2.4–3 m (8–10 ft) apart in two rows and with 3.6–4.5 m (12–15 ft) between them. Once trees have grown to 3–3.6 m (10–12 ft) high, cut off the lower branches and train the upper ones along strong wires. Prune the framework of branches in autumn or winter.

Clip and prune to form two hedges at head height

Topiary

Is topiary difficult?

Topiary was known to the Romans more than 2,000 years ago, when ships and hunting scenes were formed out of Cypress, with clipped Box used to spell names. Topiary became popular in Europe and was used formally to create spheres, squares and cones, as well as informally to depict animals. Both grand houses and cottage gardens enjoyed topiary. It is not difficult, but takes several years and regular pruning to produce an attractive feature.

FORMALITY OR FUN?

Formal topiary
Symmetrical geometric shapes

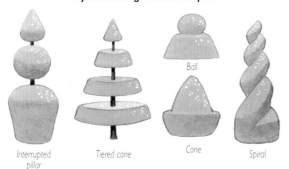

Interrupted pillar

Tiered cone

Ball

Cone

Spiral

Informal topiary
Animal or bird shapes

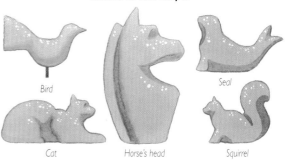

Bird

Cat

Horse's head

Seal

Squirrel

Topiary has an immediate influence on the ambience in gardens: formal geometric outlines – such as cones, pillars, pyramids, cubes, interrupted cones, spirals and balls – create stateliness and an alertness to the surrounds, while images of birds and animals have a more restful and amusing nature. Traditionally, many cottage gardens included an animal clipped in Box and peering out from borders or alongside a boundary. These features still attract attention.

Imaginative topiary can be created – but it takes several years. Here the topiary is highlighted by a surround of pea-shingle.

Range of plants

In Britain in the 1600s, plants such as Thrift, Hyssop, Lavender, Germander and Thyme were used for topiary, as well as more traditional woody plants like Box. Nowadays, many types of shrubs and trees, including conifers, are used, including the following.

- *Buxus sempervirens* (Box)
- *Cupressus macrocarpa* (Monterey Cypress)
- *Cupressus sempervirens* (Italian Cypress)
- *Ilex aquifolium* (Holly)
- *Laurus nobilis* (Bay)
- *Lonicera nitida* (Chinese Honeysuckle)
- *Myrtus communis* (Myrtle)
- *Phillyrea angustifolia*
- *Taxus baccata* (Yew)
- *Thuja plicata* (Western Red Cedar)

GETTING STARTED

Topiary is an art that needs patience and dedication, as it may take several years to produce a recognizable shape, even at its simplest. Creating a simple box outline when using *Lonicera nitida* (Chinese Honeysuckle) or *Buxus sempervirens* (Box) could take 3–4 years, while to produce the same shape and size in *Taxus baccata* (Yew) would probably demand at least twice that time, or even more.

When starting with topiary, do not be too ambitious; it is more satisfactory to produce a simple cone shape than a rabbit that rather resembles a hedgehog or kangaroo!

CREATING A CONE

This is a simple shape, but when executed perfectly creates an admired feature, either in a garden or in a tub or large pot on a patio. The easiest way to create a cone is to buy an established *Buxus sempervirens* (Box) plant and, over a couple of seasons, clip it to shape. To produce a cone will take several seasons.

The first step is to use secateurs to clip the plant to shape. By the following year, it will have produced many new shoots and at this stage it is useful to form 3–4 long canes into a wigwam shape, over and around the plant. These create a guide to the angle at which to clip the shrub. Use secateurs to cut the stems to shape. By the following year, the shape will have been formed and garden shears can be used to clip the cone several times each summer.

Tie the canes at the plant's top

Carefully clip the young shoots

Trim the young shoots

1 *Buy an established Box plant and use secateurs to shape the plant into an approximate cone. Alternatively, use hedging shears if they are easier to use.*

2 *During the following year, use 3–4 straight canes to form a cone shape. Use wires to ensure that the canes are held securely.*

3 *Use sharp hedging shears to clip the plant carefully to a cone outline. It may be necessary to clip over it several times.*

CREATING A TOPIARY BIRD

First produce a cone (see above), with a cluster of unpruned shoots at its top. Small-leaved shrubs are best and these include *Buxus sempervirens* (Box) and *Lonicera nitida* (Chinese Honeysuckle). Form two strong and equal clusters of shoots; use one to create the tail and the other to create the body and head.

Drive a strong bamboo cane vertically into the cone's centre and into the ground, so that its top is just below the cone's top. Attach to this a supporting wire framework, around which the shape of the bird can be created. Take a piece of thick wire, about 75 cm (2½ ft) long, and form a loop that will be the tail and part of the body. Use another piece of wire, about 45 cm (18 in) long, and create a loop about 7.5 cm (3 in) wide and facing at a right angle to the main piece of the wire. Then, with a slight curve, fix it to the cane. This will provide a shape for the head, and should be about 10 cm (4 in) below the top of the wire that forms the tail.

Tie bunches of shoots to each of the frameworks. Thereafter, it is a matter of regularly cutting back the shoots (not into old wood) to encourage bushiness.

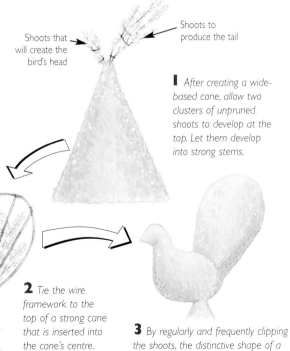

Shoots that will create the bird's head

Shoots to produce the tail

1 *After creating a wide-based cone, allow two clusters of unpruned shoots to develop at the top. Let them develop into strong stems.*

Form a loop in the wire

Tie the shoots to the wire

2 *Tie the wire framework to the top of a strong cane that is inserted into the cone's centre.*

3 *By regularly and frequently clipping the shoots, the distinctive shape of a bird, with a large tail, can be created.*

Roses

Do I need to prune my roses every year?

Roses are deciduous shrubs that need yearly pruning to encourage the regular development of flowers and to keep plants healthy and long-lived. All roses need to be pruned, whether bushes, climbers or ramblers, although it is mainly bushes such as Hybrid Tea (Large-flowered roses) and Floribunda (Cluster-flowered roses) that are the most popular types. Regrettably, a mystique about pruning roses has developed, but really it is quite simple.

PHILOSOPHY OF PRUNING BUSH ROSES

Hybrid Tea and Floribunda roses produce their best flowers on shoots that developed earlier in the same season. The size and number of new shoots these bush roses develop each year is influenced by the degree of severity by which they are pruned. For example, the further back along their length shoots are cut, the fewer the new shoots later produced, but these will be stronger.

The severity by which shoots are cut needs to take into account the vigour of the variety, the fertility of soil, whether blooms are needed for garden display or exhibition purposes, and the age of the bush. As rose bushes age, when cut back hard they produce new shoots less freely.

'Masquerade' is a vigorous and branching Floribunda rose, with yellow flowers that change to pink and red.

PRUNING HYBRID TEA AND FLORIBUNDA ROSES

Getting the timing right is important, and every rose expert has a particular opinion about this. However, the consensus is that established bushes, as well as roses planted in autumn and winter, are best pruned in early spring, just when growth is beginning but before the leaves appear. Bushes that are planted in spring are best pruned immediately after planting is completed.

In exposed areas – and especially if a bush is not fully established in the soil – bushes often become buffeted by strong winter winds that rock and loosen roots in the soil. To prevent this happening, in early winter cut back the upper parts of long stems; in spring, these will be pruned more severely.

The severity of pruning is classified as light, moderate or hard.

- **Light pruning** is ideal for bush roses growing on light, sandy soil that is low in fertility and unable to support masses of vigorous shoots. However, if this technique is used every year, bushes become tall and spindly and with poor-quality blooms. There is,

'Priscilla Burton' displays semi-double, slightly fragrant, deep carmine flowers with white eyes. It has a charming, old-fashioned nature that appeals to many rose lovers.

therefore, a need to feed and water plants regularly, and to mulch around them with well-decomposed organic material such as garden compost or farmyard manure. Then, once the bush is growing strongly, more vigorous pruning can take place. However, light pruning is a way of restraining the growth of vigorous-growing varieties such as 'Peace'.

- **Moderate pruning** suits most bush roses growing on moderately fertile soil; but if Hybrid Tea types become too tall, with a leggy nature, prune them hard every few seasons. This is the method used for most Hybrid Tea and Floribunda roses.
- **Hard pruning** is ideal for rejuvenating neglected Hybrid Tea roses, but is not suitable for established Floribunda types, as it would initiate excessive growth. However, it is recommended for newly planted bush roses and for Hybrid Tea types grown for exhibition, which demands long, strong, healthy, straight stems.

STEP-BY-STEP PRUNING

1 The first task is to cut out damaged and diseased shoots. Stems with canker can easily be seen – sunken, purplish or brownish areas usually surrounded by flaking or cracked bark. Shoots infected in this way must be cut back to healthy shoots below the point of infection.

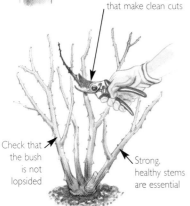

Always use sharp secateurs that make clean cuts

2 Cut out thin and weak shoots, as well as those that cross the bush's centre, create congestion and prevent the entry of light and air. Also cut out shoots that rub against each other.

Check that the bush is not lopsided

Strong, healthy stems are essential

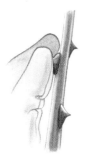

3 Cut out unripe stems, which, if left on the bush, would be damaged by severe weather. A test for the maturity of shoots is to snap off several thorns. If they cleanly break away from the stem, the wood is mature. If they tear or bend, the shoot is not mature and the shoot should be cut back to sound wood. Then, 'light', 'moderate' or 'hard' prune your rose bush (see right).

DEADHEADING AND DISBUDDING

If left, dead flowers encourage the presence of diseases

Cut to just above a leaf-joint

Bend the bud and its stem sideways

Do not damage the main stem

In addition to regular pruning, there are two other techniques used to improve the quality and size of flowers – deadheading and disbudding.
Deadheading (above left) ~ Remove all dead flowers. Cut stems back to just above a leaf-joint. Always use sharp secateurs that cut cleanly.
Disbudding (above right) ~ Many Hybrid Tea roses have shoots with more than one flower bud. To produce large, exhibition-type flowers, nip out the smaller side buds. Hold the stem while disbudding.

PRUNING BUSH ROSES

BEFORE   **Light pruning**

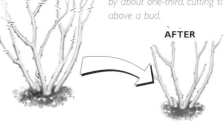

↙ ↘ *Light pruning, also known as long or high pruning, involves cutting the tops of shoots back by about one-third, cutting to just above a bud.*

AFTER

BEFORE   **Moderate pruning**

↙ ↘ *Moderate pruning, also known as medium pruning, requires cutting back stems by about a half of their length. Additionally, cut weak shoots hard back.*

AFTER

BEFORE   **Hard pruning**

↙ ↘ *Hard pruning, also known as low pruning, involves cutting all stems back to 3–4 buds, leaving stems around 13–15 cm (5–6 in) high.*

AFTER

Getting the cuts right

It is essential that the position of a cut in relation to a bud is correct. If it is too high it encourages the end of the shoot to die back; if too low it may damage the bud. The perfect cut is about 6 mm (¼ in) above the bud and with a slight slant.

WRONG CUT

Slanting cut leaves the bud exposed and likely to be knocked off

Cut too close to the bud, which is likely to have been damaged by the cut

Patio and miniature roses

Patio and miniature roses differ in size, with few miniature varieties growing taller than 38 cm (15 in) tall. Patio types, sometimes known as Dwarf Cluster-flowered Bush roses, are larger and usually 45–60 cm (1½–2 ft) high, although a few only reach 38 cm (15 in) high. Both types can be pruned in the same way as Hybrid Tea roses, but they have a more twiggy nature. Usually, they need little pruning – for details of their treatment, see below.

PRUNING MINIATURE ROSES

In mild areas, these can be pruned in autumn. In regions where the weather is frosty and cold throughout winter, leave pruning until late winter. However, if pruning is delayed until late winter, in late autumn cut back some of the top growth, so that the area exposed to buffeting wind is reduced.

The first stage is to cut out diseased and damaged shoots. Then, remove twiggy growth and cut back vigorous shoots by about a half. Ensure that the centre of the bush is not congested with stems. On very small varieties, it is sometimes easier to use a pair of sharp scissors, rather than secateurs.

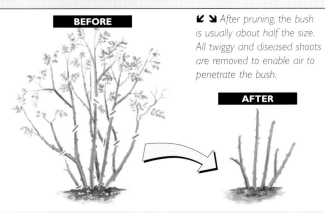

BEFORE

AFTER

↙ ↘ *After pruning, the bush is usually about half the size. All twiggy and diseased shoots are removed to enable air to penetrate the bush.*

PRUNING PATIO ROSES

'Sweet Dreams' is ideal for planting alongside patios.

These are low-growing Floribunda roses and therefore can be pruned in the same way. As with miniature roses, if the weather is harsh, leave pruning until late winter; but, in windswept areas, trim off some of the shoots in autumn to reduce the risk of plants being rocked in the soil.

Prune patio roses slightly less severely than Floribunda types, as hard pruning encourages the development of a few, strong shoots at the expense of the production of flowers.

PRUNING GROUND-COVER ROSES

These are roses with long, sprawling shoots that can be trained to cover the soil's surface. However, they do not create a total blanket over the soil and therefore do not suppress weed growth. Nevertheless, they create an attractive feature. Incidentally, the ground-cover rose 'Hertfordshire' can also be planted in a hanging-basket for display on a patio. Other ground-cover varieties include 'Essex' (reddish-pink), 'Gwent' (lemon-yellow), 'Hampshire' (glowing scarlet) and 'Wiltshire' (rosy-pink).

Cut to just beyond an upward-facing bud

↗ *Use sharp secateurs to cut out stems that intrude on other plants.*

Little pruning is needed for ground-cover roses, as they have an informal and sprawling nature. However, where they intrude on other plants, cut them back in late winter; sever stems just beyond upward-facing buds. Where a plant has a more upright and shrub-like nature, prune it as for a bush rose. Always remove faded flowers (see page 51) to encourage the development of further blooms.

Rose hedges

There are usually few difficulties with pruning a hedge. A wide range of rose types are used, including the vigorous Floribunda 'The Queen Elizabeth', Rugosas and Musks, as well as miniature types. Large hedges need space in which to develop, so do not plant them close to a boundary, as invariably they trespass on paths and pavements; pruning them just to restrict their size will mean the loss of flowers. Try planting miniature types alongside a path.

Are rose hedges difficult to prune?

PLANTING AND PRUNING ROSE HEDGES

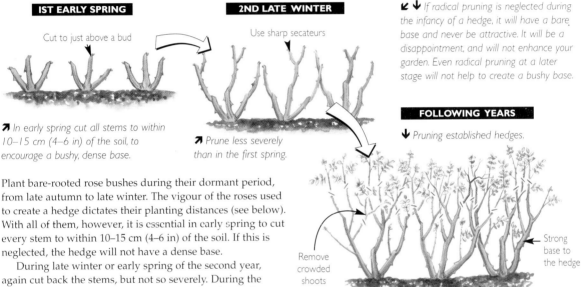

IST EARLY SPRING

Cut to just above a bud

↗ *In early spring cut all stems to within 10–15 cm (4–6 in) of the soil, to encourage a bushy, dense base.*

2ND LATE WINTER

Use sharp secateurs

↗ *Prune less severely than in the first spring.*

↙ ↓ *If radical pruning is neglected during the infancy of a hedge, it will have a bare base and never be attractive. It will be a disappointment, and will not enhance your garden. Even radical pruning at a later stage will not help to create a bushy base.*

FOLLOWING YEARS

↓ *Pruning established hedges.*

Remove crowded shoots

Strong base to the hedge

Plant bare-rooted rose bushes during their dormant period, from late autumn to late winter. The vigour of the roses used to create a hedge dictates their planting distances (see below). With all of them, however, it is essential in early spring to cut every stem to within 10–15 cm (4–6 in) of the soil. If this is neglected, the hedge will not have a dense base.

During late winter or early spring of the second year, again cut back the stems, but not so severely. During the following years, little pruning is needed other than to keep them shapely, removing crowded or dead wood. If the hedge becomes bare of leaves and colour at its base, cut a few shoots down to within 30–45 cm (12–18 in) of the soil.

Too often, attempts are made to create a hedge with an even and level top. With roses, this is impossible, and it is much better to produce a hedge with a natural, irregular outline. They should have an informal appearance.

Miniature hedges

Low hedges that have been formed from miniature rose types are better grown as internal garden divisions rather than as external boundaries. They are ideal for planting alongside paths, as well as bordering patios and other paved areas.

THE RIGHT ROSE FOR YOUR HEDGE

The selection of varieties depends on the desired height of the hedge

HEIGHT OF HEDGE	RECOMMENDED VARIETIES
Low hedges *Up to 75 cm (2½ ft) high and planted 30–38 cm (12–15 in) apart in a single row*	These are formed mainly of miniature, patio and dwarf Polyanthas and include varieties such as 'White Pet' (white and also known as 'Little White Pet'), 'Marlena' (scarlet-crimson) and 'The Fairy' (rose-pink).
Medium-height hedges *75 cm–1.5 m (2½–5 ft) high and planted 45 cm (18 in) apart in single or double rows*	These are formed of varieties such as 'Iceberg' (white) and 'Masquerade' (yellow, red and pink).
Tall hedges *1.5–2.1 m (5–7 ft) high and planted 75–90 cm (2½–3 ft) apart in a single row*	These are formed of varieties such as 'Felicia' (silvery-pink), 'Penelope' (pink, flushed apricot) and 'The Queen Elizabeth' (pink).

Standard roses.

How do I prune a standard rose?

Good positions for a standard rose are among bush roses, as a centrepiece in an island bed or alongside a path. Full standards, with their added height, are better than half-standards for planting among bush roses. Pruning is not difficult, although regular attention is needed to ensure that the head does not become too large and thereby buffeted by strong wind. Both Hybrid Tea and Floribunda varieties are grown as standards and half-standards.

THE RANGE OF STANDARD ROSES

It is always best to buy a standard rose, rather than attempting to raise your own. The best standards will have two – sometimes three – buds budded onto the rootstock, and this creates a plant with an evenly shaped head.

- Standard roses will have been budded 90 cm (3 ft) above the ground, and this forms heads that are 1.5–1.8 m (5–6 ft) high.
- Half-standard roses are budded 75 cm (2½ ft) above the ground, and this forms heads that are 1.3–1.6 m (4½–5½ ft) high.
- Weeping standards are budded 1.3 m (4½ ft) above the ground, and the head is 1.5–1.8 m (5–6 ft) high.

Range of standard roses

In addition to many Hybrid Tea and Floribunda roses, others can be used. These include New English Roses such as 'Anne Boleyn', 'Golden Celebration', 'Graham Thomas', 'Molineux', 'Portmeirion' and 'Winchester Cathedral'. Old Rose varieties include 'De Meaux', 'Officinalis' and Rosa Mundi (Rosa gallica 'Versicolor').

Rosa Mundi (Rosa gallica *Versicolor) makes a superb standard rose.*

PLANTING AND PRUNING STANDARD ROSES

I Plant a bare-rooted standard rose during its dormant period, from late autumn to late winter, and ensure that it is firmly supported by a stake. In late winter or early spring, cut back strong stems to 3–5 buds from the point where they were budded.

WIND RISK

In exposed gardens, wind is the greatest hazard to standard roses. If possible, only plant standard roses in sheltered positions or where the wind's speed has been reduced by hedges.

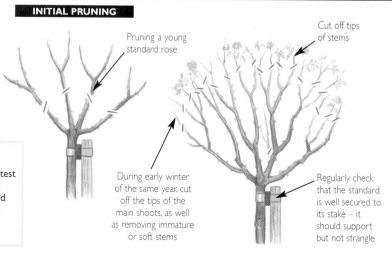

INITIAL PRUNING

Pruning a young standard rose

Cut off tips of stems

During early winter of the same year, cut off the tips of the main shoots, as well as removing immature or soft stems

Regularly check that the standard is well secured to its stake – it should support but not strangle

PLANTING AND PRUNING STANDARD ROSES (CONTINUED)

FOLLOWING YEAR

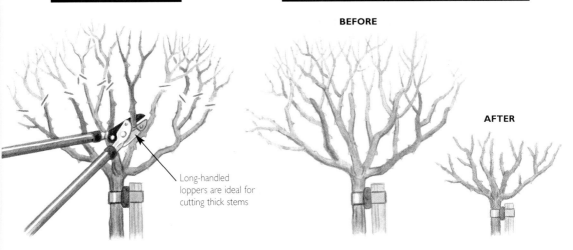

Long-handled loppers are ideal for cutting thick stems

PRUNING AN ESTABLISHED STANDARD ROSE

BEFORE

AFTER

2 In late winter of the following year, cut out diseased, crossing and dead shoots. Additionally, prune back new shoots to 3–5 buds (about 15 cm/6 in) and the remaining lateral shoots to 2–4 buds (10–15 cm/4–6 in).

3 By the following late winter, the head will be formed. Cut back shoots on Hybrid Tea varieties to 3–5 buds (about 15 cm/6 in) from their base. On Floribunda varieties, cut back one-year-old shoots to 6–8 buds (about 25 cm/10 in) and two-year-old shoots to 3–6 buds (about 15 cm/6 in). In rose terms, these buds are sometimes known as 'eyes'. In the following years, continue pruning in the same way.

FIRM STAKING

Securely staking the main stem is important, as it will easily snap during strong winds if it is unsupported. While the standard is being planted, knock the stake into the soil, on the windward side of the tree, so that the stem will not be blown and rubbed against it. The top of the stake should be slightly below the position where the plant was budded. Use 2–3 proprietary tree-ties to secure the stem to the stake.

Wind

Regularly check that the ties are secure, holding the stem firm but not constricting or chafing it

PRUNING WEEPING STANDARDS

These are the rose equivalents of crinolines, as they produce a colourful, somewhat globe-like, tapestry of flowers. Many rambler varieties are used to create this eye-catching feature, including 'Albéric Barbier' (cream), 'Crimson Shower' (red), 'François Juranville' (salmon-pink), 'Goldfinch' (yellow, fading to white) and 'Sander's White Rambler' (white).

Pruning weeping standards is relatively simple. The initial pruning is relatively severe; in late winter or early spring after being planted cut back all shoots to about 15 cm (6 in) long. This encourages the development of strong shoots. Once the head is formed, all that is needed in early autumn is to cut out shoots that produced flowers during the current season. This will leave young shoots that will bear flowers during the following year. If there are insufficient young shoots to bear flowers during the following year, leave a few of the older shoots in place and cut back their sideshoots to 2–3 buds to help create a fuller head.

To enable shoots to be trained in an even and cascading manner, a rose-trainer can be fitted to the top of the stake at an early time in the growth of the standard. These trainers are available in several sizes: 60 cm (2 ft), 75 cm (2½ ft) and 90 cm (3 ft) wide.

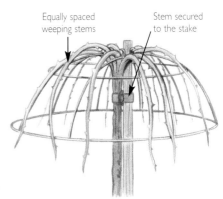

Equally spaced weeping stems

Stem secured to the stake

Creating an evenly shaped head for a weeping standard is made easier by the use of a rose-trainer. This should be fitted at an early stage.

Shrub roses

Do I need to prune my shrub rose?

Although shrub roses have a relaxed nature, they need regular pruning to prevent congestion and to ensure longevity. It is often thought that, because shrub roses have been grown without any human help for several thousand years, pruning is not necessary. This may suit some of them, but not all. The way your shrub rose is pruned also depends on its type. They can be divided into three main pruning groups – these are described and illustrated below.

PLANTING AND PRUNING GROUP ONE

These are roses that have a dense, twiggy nature and bear flowers mainly on sub-lateral shoots, as well as on short laterals. Once established, they do not often produce vigorous shoots from their base. This group includes:

- Hybrid Musks, which bear flowers in large clusters
- *Rosa gallica* (French Rose)
- *Rosa pimpinellifolia* (Scotch Rose/Burnet Rose) and its hybrids
- *Rosa rugosa* (Ramanas Rose/Japanese Rose) and its hybrids
- Species roses (but not climbers) and their close hybrids

When planted as bare-rooted plants during their dormant period, cut off damaged roots and shorten unripe shoots. During the first year, cut out diseased and thin shoots in winter.

I During late winter or early spring of the second year, cut out badly positioned shoots that have developed from the plant's base. Also cut back the tips of vigorous shoots. During summer, the plant will bear flowers. Cut these off as soon as they fade, as well as thin and weak shoots.

Cut out badly positioned shoots

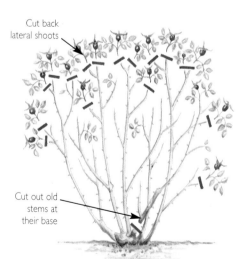

Cut back lateral shoots

Cut out old stems at their base

2 During the third and subsequent years, in late winter or early spring, cut back lateral shoots. Also cut out at their base 1–2 shoots that are past their best.

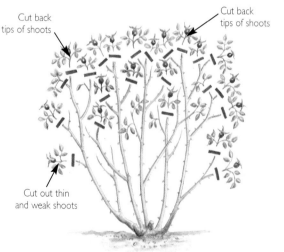

Cut back tips of shoots

Cut back tips of shoots

Cut out thin and weak shoots

3 In each autumn, cut back the tips of shoots to encourage the development of lateral shoots. These are the ones that will mainly bear flowers during the following year. Also cut out weak and thin shoots, as well as a few old shoots from the plant's base.

PLANTING AND PRUNING GROUP TWO

These are roses that chiefly flower on short lateral shoots, as well as from sub-lateral shoots growing from wood that is two or more years old. This group includes:

- Modern Shrub Roses which do not have a repeat-flowering nature and have only one main flush of flowers in mid-summer
- Moss Roses
- most Damask Roses (*Rosa damascena*)
- *Rosa* x *alba* types
- *Rosa* x *centifolia* (Provence Rose) and its types

When planted as bare-rooted plants during their dormant period, cut off any damaged roots and shorten unripe shoots. During the first year, cut out all diseased and thin shoots in winter.

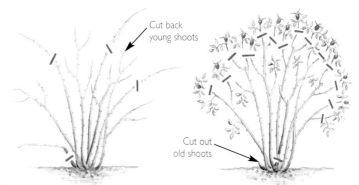

Cut back young shoots

Cut out old shoots

1 In late winter or early spring of the second year, cut back by about one-third young shoots growing from the plant's base. Also cut out badly positioned shoots, and lateral shoots to 2–3 buds. During the following summer, flowers will appear on the cut-back laterals. In autumn, cut back the tips of shoots that are extra long.

2 In late winter and early spring, and during subsequent years, cut back by one-third all new shoots that grew from ground level. Also cut back laterals on flowered shoots to 2–3 buds from their base, and cut out a few old shoots to enable light and air to enter the plant. Later in the same season, in autumn, cut off the tips of extra long shoots.

PLANTING AND PRUNING GROUP THREE

These are roses that have a similar flowering nature to those in Group Two, but with a slight difference. They have a nearly recurrent-flowering nature, throughout summer and into autumn. They bear flowers on the current season's shoots as well as on lateral and sub-lateral shoots. Also, these plants often develop long shoots from their base or on strong stems slightly higher up. This group includes:

- vigorous Hybrid Perpetuals and Hybrid Tea roses
- many Modern Shrub Roses, other than those detailed in Group Two (see above)
- most China Roses

When planted as bare-rooted plants during their dormant period, cut off damaged roots and shorten unripe shoots. During the first year, cut out thin shoots in winter.

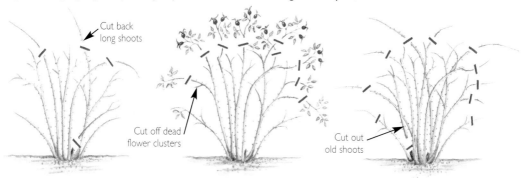

Cut back long shoots

Cut off dead flower clusters

Cut out old shoots

1 During late winter or early spring, cut back by about one-third excessively long shoots that have grown from the shrub's base. Cut back laterals on shoots which flowered during the previous season to 2–3 buds from their base, and also completely cut out any weak and thin shoots.

2 During summer, the bush will bear flowers; cut off dead clusters in late summer or early autumn. In late autumn, cut back the tips of long shoots.

3 In late winter or early spring of the following year – and all subsequent years – cut back by about one-third long shoots that grow from the shrub's base. Cut back lateral shoots that flowered during the previous year to 2–3 buds. In addition, completely cut out weak and spindly shoots. In late summer or early autumn, cut off dead flowers; in late autumn cut back the tips of long shoots.

Climbing roses

Is it easy to prune climbers?

How you prune a climbing rose is dictated by the type of climber you have. In general, climbers have a permanent or semi-permanent framework of shoots and it is from lateral shoots that flowers are borne. These shoots develop in spring and summer and bear flowers during the same year. There are several types of climber and they can be divided into two main groups, according to the way they are pruned. These varieties are listed below.

ORIGINS OF CLIMBING ROSES

Climbers are derived from several sources: some are natural climbers, a few are sports (natural changes) of Hybrid Tea or Floribunda varieties, while others have a more complex ancestry. Climbers are the traditional roses for clothing walls in summer colour. They are not self-supporting and require a framework to which they can be attached. Ensure that the supporting framework is well secured to the wall, using strong 'fixings'.

The climbing Hybrid Tea 'Meg' creates a distinctive feature, displaying pink flowers with an apricot base. It has a relaxed nature and is ideal for growing against old walls.

PRUNING GROUPS

Group One
Varieties include:
- 'Casino' (pale yellow)
- 'Climbing Ena Harkness' (crimson-scarlet)
- 'Climbing Etoile de Hollande' (deep red)
- 'Madame Grégoire Staechelin' (pink, shaded crimson)
- 'Mermaid' (primrose-yellow)
- 'Parkdirektor Riggers' (blood-red)

Group Two
Varieties include:
- 'Aloha' (rose-pink)
- 'Altissimo' (red)
- 'Bantry Bay' (rose-pink)
- 'Breath of Life' (apricot)

- 'Climbing Cécile Brünner' (shell-pink')
- 'Climbing Crimson Glory' (crimson)
- 'Climbing Iceberg' (white)
- 'Climbing Lady Sylvia' (pale pink)
- 'Climbing Masquerade' (yellow, then pink and red)
- 'Climbing Mrs Sam McGredy' (coppery-orange)
- 'Climbing Super Star' (orange-vermilion)
- 'Compassion' (pink, shaded apricot)
- 'Danse du Feu' (orange-scarlet)
- 'Dortmund' (red, with a white eye)
- 'Galway Bay' (pink)

- 'Gloire de Dijon' (buff-yellow)
- 'Golden Showers' (golden-yellow)
- 'Guinée' (dark red)
- 'Handel' (cream, edged pink)
- 'Highfield' (pale yellow)
- 'Leverkusen' (pale yellow)
- 'Madame Alfred Carrière' (white, flushed pink)
- 'Maigold' (bronze-yellow)
- 'Meg' (pink, with apricot base)
- 'Morning Jewel' (pink)
- 'Pink Perpétué' (rose-pink)
- 'Rose Mantle' (deep rose-pink)
- 'Royal Gold' (deep yellow)

- 'Schoolgirl' (apricot-yellow)
- 'Swan Lake' (white, tinged pink)
- 'White Cockade' (white)
- 'Zéphirine Drouhin' (carmine-pink)

Climbers that cannot be identified

You may have a climber that is not on this list. If it flowers mainly on lateral shoots, treat it as a plant in Group One.

PRUNING NEWLY PLANTED CLIMBERS

Plant bare-rooted specimens during their dormant period, from late autumn to late winter. In spring, cut out dead wood, especially the tips of stems that have been damaged by frost. Secure the stems to a supporting framework, so that rain and wind cannot damage them. Ensure that the stems are firmly supported, but not strangled. Do not be tempted to cut down the stems after the climber has been planted; unlike for a rambling rose (which initially is radically pruned), the stems on climbers are left alone. In autumn, use sharp secateurs to cut off dead flowers.

SELECTING A CLIMBER

Climbing roses create a permanent framework of stems and shoots. These are secured to a supporting framework, and therefore once selected and planted it is more difficult than with ramblers to remove and replant with another variety. Therefore, take care that the right variety is planted. There are many varieties to choose from and a range is listed on the opposite page.

PRUNING GROUP ONE

Prune established roses in late winter or early spring. Little pruning is needed, other than the removal of dead wood and withered shoot tips. Lateral shoots which produced flowers during the previous year need to be cut back to about 7.5 cm (3 in) long.

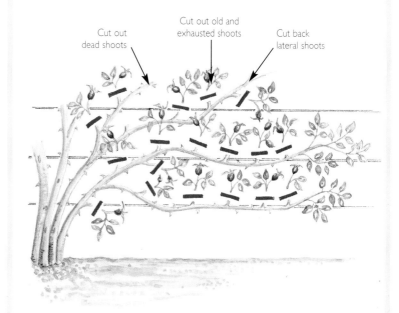

Cut out dead shoots

Cut out old and exhausted shoots

Cut back lateral shoots

↗ *Pruning is relatively simple and the above illustration shows how to prune varieties in Group One. Nevertheless, it ensures the regular production of flowers.*

PRUNING GROUP TWO

Prune established roses in late winter or early spring. Little pruning is needed – less than for those in Group One. Cut out dead shoots, as well as withered shoot tips. Do not prune lateral shoots.

→ *To maintain a regular and yearly display of flowers it is essential to prune a climber each year.*

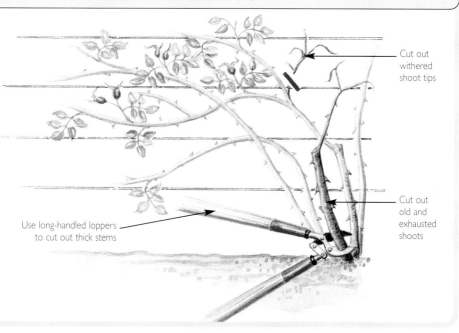

Cut out withered shoot tips

Cut out old and exhausted shoots

Use long-handled loppers to cut out thick stems

Rambling roses

Do ramblers need severe pruning?

The stems on newly planted ramblers need radical pruning. This is because, unlike climbers, they develop long, flexible stems and do not have a permanent framework. Their flowers are borne on shoots which developed during the previous year. This indicates the basic pruning technique; as soon as they finish flowering, these shoots are cut out. For detailed pruning purposes, ramblers are divided into three groups (see below for relevant varieties).

ORIGINS OF RAMBLING ROSES

Ramblers are derived from several sources: Multiflora Hybrids have small flowers borne in large trusses on stiff growths, whereas Sempervirens Hybrids are graceful, with long, slender, but strong stems, and with small flowers borne in sprays. Wichuraiana Hybrids, which encompasses the majority of ramblers, are graceful with large flowers in elegant sprays. In addition to these groups, there are also other superb ramblers, including Banksians and Boursaults.

None of these ramblers is self-supporting, and therefore all require a framework to which they can be attached.

'American Pillar' is a delightful rambler that will provide masses of colour.

PLANTING AND PRUNING RAMBLERS

Plant bare-rooted ramblers from late autumn to late winter. Sometimes the stems have been shortened by the nursery before despatch. However, before planting them, cut all shoots back to 23–38 cm (9–15 in) long. Also cut back damaged and coarse roots. Plant the rambler slightly deeper than before, and firm friable soil over and around the roots. During spring, young shoots will grow from the tops of the shoots and later create a colourful array of flowers.

Pruning groups

Group One
Varieties include:
- 'American Pillar'
  (deep pink, with white eye)
- 'Crimson Shower' (crimson)
- 'Dorothy Perkins' (rose-pink)
- 'Excelsa'
  (rosy-crimson, with white centre)
- 'François Juranville' (pale pink)
- 'Sander's White Rambler' (white)
- 'Seagull' (white)

Group Two
Varieties include:
- 'Albéric Barbier' (cream)
- 'Albertine' (pale pink)
- 'Paul's Scarlet Climber' (scarlet)
- 'Veilchenblau'
  (violet, shading to slate-grey)

Group Three
Varieties include:
- 'Emily Gray' (buff-yellow)
- *Rosa filipes* 'Kiftsgate' (creamy-white)
- 'Wedding Day' (creamy-white)

PRUNING GROUP ONE

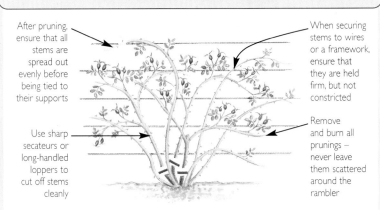

After pruning, ensure that all stems are spread out evenly before being tied to their supports

When securing stems to wires or a framework, ensure that they are held firm, but not constricted

Use sharp secateurs or long-handled loppers to cut off stems cleanly

Remove and burn all prunings – never leave them scattered around the rambler

Prune established ramblers in autumn, cutting down to ground level all stems that produced flowers during that season. Tie in the new stems that developed during the same year – and will produce flowers during the following year – to their supports. If the rambler has not produced many new stems, retain some of the older ones and trim their lateral stems to about 7.5 cm (3 in) long.

Sometimes it is difficult to sort out the canes, as they may have developed into a near thicket. If this happens, just cut back lateral shoots to 7.5 cm (3 in) from the main stems.

PRUNING GROUP TWO

Prune established ramblers in autumn, cutting all shoots that produced flowers back to a point where new and vigorous shoots have developed. Also cut back 1–2 old stems to 30–38 cm (12–15 in) above the soil.

As with Group One, sometimes it is difficult to sort out the canes. In this case, just cut back lateral shoots to 7.5 cm (3 in) from the main stems.

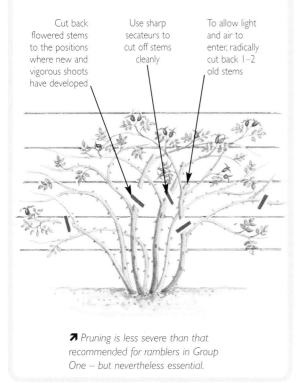

Cut back flowered stems to the positions where new and vigorous shoots have developed

Use sharp secateurs to cut off stems cleanly

To allow light and air to enter, radically cut back 1–2 old stems

↗ Pruning is less severe than that recommended for ramblers in Group One – but nevertheless essential.

PRUNING GROUP THREE

Pruning established ramblers in this group is easy. In autumn, prune them lightly, cutting out old and dead wood and the tips of lateral shoots that have flowered.

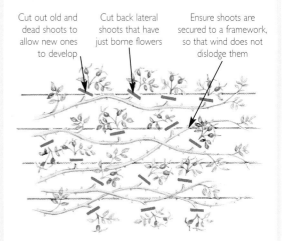

Cut out old and dead shoots to allow new ones to develop

Cut back lateral shoots that have just borne flowers

Ensure shoots are secured to a framework, so that wind does not dislodge them

↗ Of the three different pruning regimes, this is the simplest and easiest to undertake. Nevertheless, it is an essential part of growing these rambling varieties.

PRUNING A PILLAR ROSE

Pillar roses are useful for creating height and focal points in a garden – and are relatively inexpensive to create. They form beacons of interest and are easy to create and prune. Erect a support, about 2.4 m (8 ft) high, formed of a rustic pole with its branches cut to leave 15–20 cm (6–8 in) stubs. These stubs give support to the rose's stems and help to prevent them falling sideways.

Plant bare-rooted pillar roses from late autumn to late winter. Tie the long stems to the pole. During summer, lateral shoots will develop on the stems. Cut off the flowers as soon as they have faded. In early winter, cut back the laterals that produced flowers, at the same time removing all weak, diseased and thin shoots.

During the following summer (and in all subsequent years), the lateral shoots on the old wood will bear flowers. Cut these off when they fade, and in early winter cut back the laterals that produced the flowers.

'Paul's Scarlet Climber' is ideal for growing up a pillar or other rustic support like this 'wigwam'.

Apples

Why prune apple trees?

The objective when pruning an apple tree is to build up the plant's shape – whether it is a bush, tree, cordon, pyramid or espalier – so that it can bear fruits regularly, each year and for many years. Creating a framework of well-spaced branches may take 4–5 years when starting with a maiden tree. Other purposes of pruning are to encourage the development of fruit buds and to regulate their positions and numbers on the branches of the tree.

TIP- OR SPUR-BEARING?

> ### Key
> **C** = culinary type (cooking apple)
> **D** = dessert type (eating apple)

There are two main ways in which apples bear fruits: a few varieties produce fruits in both of these styles.

- **Tip-bearing types** produce fruits on fruit buds on or near the tips of shoots. Varieties that bear fruits in this way include 'Beauty of Bath' (D), 'Irish Peach' (D) and 'Worcester Pearmain' (D).
- **Spur-bearing types** develop fruits mainly on fruit buds on short spurs close to the branch. Varieties that bear fruits in this way include 'Ashmead Kernel' (D), 'Cox's Orange Pippin' (D), 'Discovery' (D), 'Egremont Russet' (D), 'Ellison's Orange' (D), 'Epicure' (D), 'George Neal' (C), 'Golden Delicious' (D), 'Grenadier' (C), 'Howgate Wonder' (C), 'Idared' (D), 'James Grieve' (D), 'Kidd's Orange Red' (D), 'Lane's Prince Albert' (C), 'Orlean's Reinette' (D), 'Ribston Pippin' (D), 'Sunset' (D) and 'Tydeman's Late Orange' (D).
- **Tip/spur-bearing varieties** include 'Bramley's Seedling' (C), 'George Cave' (D), 'Golden Noble' (C), 'Lord Lambourne' (D) and 'St Edmund's Russet' (D). These varieties are best pruned as for spur-bearing types.

This apple tree (a 'Cox's Orange Pippin') is bearing a heavy crop of fruits. To reduce the risk of damage to its branches, they are supported in a 'maypole' manner.

'Cox's Orange Pippin' bears its fruits on spurs. Therefore, it is essential that pruning is directed towards encouraging the development of plenty of fruiting spurs.

GROWING BUSH APPLES

Apples can be grown in several ways, but the simplest method is as bushes. They have stems 60–90 cm (2–3 ft) long. There are both ordinary bush forms and dwarf bush types.

- Ordinary bushes are planted 3.6–4.5 m (12–15 ft) apart and yield 27–54 kg (60–120 lb) of apples each year.
- Dwarf bushes are planted 2.4–4.5 m (8–15 ft) apart and yield 13.5–22.5 kg (30–50 lb) of apples each year. These compact bushes are ideal for planting in a small garden.

PLANTING AND PRUNING A BUSH APPLE

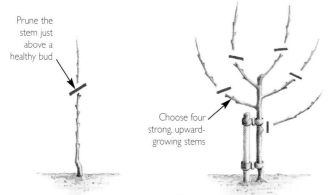

Prune the stem just above a healthy bud

Choose four strong, upward-growing stems

1 From late autumn to late winter plant bare-rooted, one-year-old trees. These will have a single stem. In winter, cut each plant back to 75 cm (2½ ft) high for an ordinary bush apple and 60 cm (2 ft) for dwarf types. Cut just above a healthy bud.

2 During the following winter, the two-year-old bush will have several strong stems that grow upwards. Select four of the strongest to form the main branches and cut them back by two-thirds. Prune each shoot to an outward-facing bud.

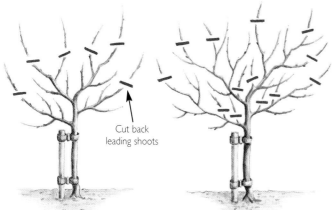

Cut back leading shoots

3 By the following winter, the three-year-old bush will have many shoots; some are extensions of the previously cut-back shoots, others are sideshoots. Cut back all leading shoots by about two-thirds and sideshoots to three buds long. Also, cut out crossing and damaged shoots.

4 By the following winter, the bush will have grown dramatically and have several leading shoots as well as sideshoots. Shorten leading shoots by one-third to a half, and cut back sideshoots to about 10 cm (4 in) long. Cut out all dead shoots and those that cross the bush's centre.

BIENNIAL BEARING VARIETIES

Some varieties, such as 'Bramley's Seedling', 'Blenheim Orange' and 'Laxton's Superb', naturally bear a heavier crop in one year than another. This cropping imbalance can be corrected. In the spring before the production of a heavy crop, rub out a half to three-quarters of the fruit buds from each spur, leaving only 1–2 fruiting buds on each. Take care not to damage those buds that remain.

PRUNING ESTABLISHED BUSHES

As with the training period, prune established bushes during winter when plants are dormant. The technique to use depends on whether the bush is tip- or spur-bearing.

- **Tip-bearing varieties** ~ It is essential each year to encourage the development of young shoots. For this reason, leave short lateral shoots unpruned so that they develop fruit buds at their tips. After a few years, they are pruned back. Cut back leading shoots by about one-third, cutting them to just above an upward-pointing bud. Also cut back to one bud shoots which are growing from the laterals.
- **Spur-bearing varieties** ~ It is essential each year to encourage the development of fruiting spurs. Shorten all lateral shoots to just above 3–4 buds from their bases. Additionally, shorten to one bud laterals that were pruned during the previous year, and cut back the leader shoot to half of the growth it produced during the previous year.

REPLACEMENT SHOOTS

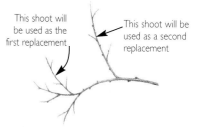

This shoot will be used as the first replacement

This shoot will be used as a second replacement

Each year the weight of fruit forces down branches. Replacement shoots help to restore and correct this tendency.

During a tree's life, the weight of fruits is continually bending down branches. Therefore, it is essential that each branch has at least one reserve shoot – further back from the shoot's tip – that can be used as a replacement as soon as the branch's tip becomes too low. During winter pruning, ensure that a replacement shoot, such as one growing upwards and near to the branch's tip, is left. When the branch becomes bent down, cut it back to the replacement shoot. Later, this replacement shoot will also need to have a replacement.

Pears

Are pears more difficult to grow than apples?

Pears are grown in exactly the same way as apples. However, pear trees live longer but are slightly more difficult to grow. This is because they flower earlier than apples and therefore the blossom is more susceptible to frost damage. Dessert pear varieties need more sun than apples and are less able to withstand drought. Additionally, their fruit buds are more attractive to birds than those of apples and therefore it may be necessary to protect them.

TIP- OR SPUR-BEARING?

Like apples, some pear varieties are tip-bearing and others are spur-bearing. With pears, it is essential that two compatible varieties (which flower at the same time) are grown near to each other to ensure cross-pollination. The following list divides varieties into groups, according to their flowering period; select at least two trees in the same group to ensure pollination. An indication is also given about whether each is tip- or spur-bearing.

Pollination Group One
- 'Beurré Hardy' (spur-bearing) dessert variety
- 'Conference' (spur-bearing) dessert variety
- 'Jargonelle' (tip-bearing) dessert variety
- 'Joséphine de Malines' (tip-bearing) dessert variety
- 'William's Bon Chrétien' (spur-bearing) dessert variety

Pollination Group Two
- 'Clapp's Favourite' (spur-bearing) dessert variety
- 'Doyenné du Comice' (spur-bearing) dessert variety
- 'Gorham' (spur-bearing) dessert variety
- 'Improved Fertility' (spur-bearing) dessert variety
- 'Pitmaston Duchess' (spur-bearing) dessert and culinary variety
- 'Winter Nelis' (spur-bearing) dessert variety

Pollination Group Three
- 'Belle Guérandaise' (spur-bearing) dessert variety
- 'Beurré Clairgeau' (spur-bearing) culinary variety
- 'Louise Bonne of Jersey' (spur-bearing) dessert variety
- 'Marguerite Marillat' (spur-bearing) dessert variety
- 'Seckel' (spur-bearing) dessert variety
- 'Vicar of Winkfield' (spur-bearing) culinary variety

The spur-bearing 'Pitmaston Duchess' is both a dessert and culinary variety, and therefore an ideal choice for home gardeners.

Pruning tip- and spur-bearing varieties

Tip-bearing ~ Prune them lightly, by cutting back only the longest laterals to four buds.

Spur-bearing ~ These bear fruits on wood that is at least two years old. Shorten new growth on leaders by about one-third and cut back lateral shoots to 3–4 buds. Shorten or remove spur systems that have become crowded. Also cut back main branches that cross the centre of the tree or each other.

PLANTING AND PRUNING AN ESPALIER PEAR

Espaliers need a strong framework of wires to which they can be secured and trained. Install strong posts, 3.6–5.4 m (12–18 ft) apart, in the soil. Intermediate supports may also be needed. Create tiers of wires, 38–45 cm (15–18 in) apart, with the lower one 38 cm (15 in) above the ground. Alternatively, secure the wires to a wall. The initial pruning and establishment of an espalier pear also can be used for apples.

I During winter, plant a bare-rooted maiden tree and prune it to about 38 cm (15 in) high and just above the first supporting wire. Cut just above a healthy bud. The top bud will later create upward growth, while two lower ones will form lateral shoots.

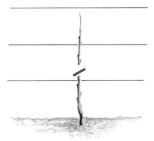

PLANTING AND PRUNING AN ESPALIER PEAR (CONTINUED)

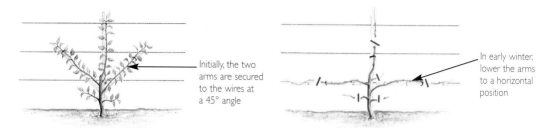

Initially, the two arms are secured to the wires at a 45° angle

In early winter, lower the arms to a horizontal position

2 During the summer of the following year, shoots will appear from the top three buds. Tie the vertical one to an upright cane, itself tied to the wires. Tie each of the two 'arms' to canes and secure them to the wires at a 45° angle.

3 In early winter, carefully lower the 'arms' to horizontal positions and tie the canes to the wires (sometimes it is recommended that the canes are removed, but for novice gardeners it is better to leave them in place). Check that the stems are not being constricted by the ties. Cut back the central shoot to just above the next tier of wire, severing the stem slightly above a healthy bud. Also cut back the lateral stems by one-third, cutting to downward-pointing buds. Where other lateral shoots have developed towards the stem's base, cut these back to three buds.

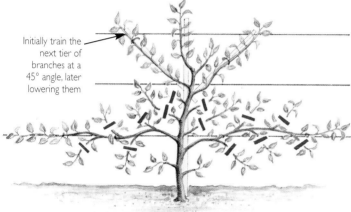

Initially train the next tier of branches at a 45° angle, later lowering them

4 During summer, new growth will be made. Train the second tier of branches in the same way as the first layer. Cut back lateral shoots from the horizontal arms to three leaves above the basal cluster. Also prune back to three leaves shoots that arise from the central stem.

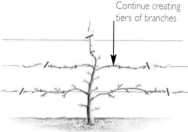

Continue creating tiers of branches

5 By the following early winter, the main stem will have created further vertical growth, and this can be cut back to just above the next tier of wires. At the same time, cut back the horizontal shoots by one-third of their new growth, again cutting to downward-pointing buds.

When the top tier of wires is reached, cut off the leading shoot

Cut back the ends of the arms, as suggested

6 As the top tier of wires is reached, cut off the central stem just above a lateral arm. Also cut back by about one-third new growth produced at the ends of the arms.

Plums and gages

How do I grow plums and gages?

Plums and gages are grown in several ways, including fans, pyramids and half-standards, but the easiest method is as bushes. They are not suitable for growing as cordons or espaliers. Once established, bushes require little pruning and this makes them ideal fruits for busy gardeners. When grown as a bush, ensure that the rootstock is St Julien A, spacing plants 6 m (20 ft) apart, or, preferably, Pixy, spacing plants 3.6–4.5 m (12–15 ft) apart.

Plum trees need little pruning once established, and are therefore ideal for home gardens where not much time is available.

Frost danger

When choosing plum varieties, avoid those such as 'Ontario' and 'Warwickshire Drooper' that flower early and therefore have blossom that is fairly likely to be damaged by frost. It is simply a waste of space to grow frost-vulnerable varieties.

THINNING PLUMS AND SUPPORTING BRANCHES

Plum trees will produce heavy crops during some seasons, and this can cause branches to break. To overcome this problem, fruits can be thinned. When they are the size of hazelnuts and the stones have formed within them, thin them simply by picking some of the fruits.

Later, repeat this thinning when the fruits are about twice that size; leave individual fruits about 5 cm (2 in) apart.

If, as picking time approaches and the fruits reach maturity, the branches start to bow under the weight, it will be necessary to support them with strong, tall posts with forked tops; these should be pushed into the soil.

PLANTING AND PRUNING A BUSH PLUM

Plant a plum or gage during its dormant season and preferably in late autumn or early winter. Growth begins early in spring for plums and gages and pruning cannot be started until the sap starts to rise and buds break into growth. Pruning plums and gages in winter, while they are dormant, risks an infection of silver leaf. Always paint cuts with a fungicidal wound-sealing paint.

Securely stake the tree; this is best done by knocking a stake into the soil before setting the plant in position. This avoids damaging the roots. About 75 cm (2½ ft) of stake should protrude above the soil.

I Plant a two-year-old tree and use proprietary ties to secure it to a stake. In early spring, as buds are breaking into growth, cut the central stem to about 90 cm (3 ft) high and just above a healthy sideshoot. There should be three strong shoots below it that will develop into the main branches. Cut them back by a half to two-thirds and just above an outward-facing bud.

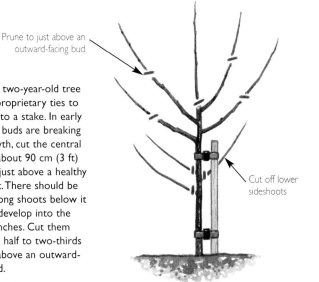

Prune to just above an outward-facing bud

Cut off lower sideshoots

PLANTING AND PRUNING A BUSH PLUM (CONTINUED)

2 During early spring of the following year, the bush will have made considerable growth. Cut back by about a half all of the new growth, severing just beyond an outward-facing bud. At the same time, cut out at their bases all other shoots growing from the main shoots. Cut off shoots that are growing from the trunk and below the lowest main branch.

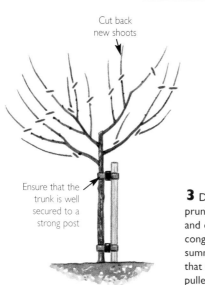

Cut back new shoots

Ensure that the trunk is well secured to a strong post

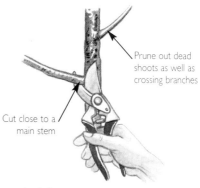

Prune out dead shoots as well as crossing branches

Cut close to a main stem

3 During the following and subsequent springs, little pruning is needed. However, cut out crossing branches and dead shoots in summer. When bushes become congested with wood, thin out some of them during summer to avoid overcrowding. Also remove suckers that are growing at the bush's base. These are best pulled off rather than being cut by secateurs. There is then less chance of further suckers growing.

CREATING A HALF-STANDARD PLUM TREE

Where space is not a consideration, grow a plum tree as a half-standard, with 6–7.5 m (20–25 ft) between trees. Such a tree will produce about 13.5–27 kg (30–60 lb) of fruits each year. In comparison, a bush will yield up to 22.5 kg (50 lb) of fruits in a good season. Half-standards enable grass around them to be cut more easily than if in bush form, as they have trunks about 1.3 m (4½ ft) high, but take care not to damage low branches.

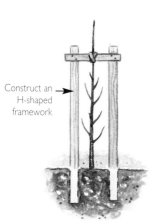

Construct an H-shaped framework

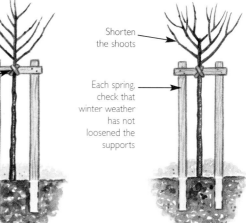

Regularly check that the tie is secure but not constrictive

Shorten the shoots

Each spring, check that winter weather has not loosened the supports

1 Plant a two-year-old tree in late autumn or early winter and secure the stem to an H-shaped framework. In early spring, as soon as growth begins and buds are bursting into life, cut back the stem to about 1.3 m (4½ ft) high. At the same time, shorten sideshoots to 7.5 cm (3 in) long. Later, these will be cut back, but initially they are useful for encouraging growth.

2 During the following early spring, select several well-spaced shoots and cut them back by half. These will form the main branches of the tree. At the same time, completely cut out all other shoots, including the ones that were left lower down on the trunk.

3 In the following spring, shorten by about a half the shoots that form the main framework. In later years, just cut out crossing and dead shoots, as well as pulling off any sucker-like shoots from the tree's base.

Peaches and nectarines

Are peaches and nectarines pruned in the same way?

These two fruits are closely related – the smooth-skinned nectarine is a form of the somewhat hairy-surfaced peach. Nectarines are slightly smaller and often have a sweeter flavour. They respond to the same pruning techniques, although nectarines are less hardy and in cold areas are frequently grown as fans against a warm, sheltered wall. However, they also can be grown as bushes, and this requires less exacting pruning, but usually takes more space.

FRUITING NATURE

Peaches and nectarines produce fruits on shoots that developed during the previous season. This means that each year it is essential to encourage the growth of new shoots to replace those that have borne fruits during the previous season.

These succulent fruits have three distinctive types of buds. Fruit buds are plump and bear fruits, while growth buds are pointed and produce shoots. There are also triple buds, which have a central fruit bud, and a growth bud on either side.

In order to encourage the development of shoots, it is essential to prune to a growth bud. However, when a growth bud is not present, instead prune to a triple bud.

JUST FOR HOT CLIMATES?

Peaches and nectarines are not just for warm countries, although in temperate regions it is best to grow a peach against a wind-sheltered wall in full sun.

'Rochester' is a popular and reliable peach. The fruits are ready for picking in the early or middle part of late summer.

PLANTING AND PRUNING A FAN-TRAINED PEACH OR NECTARINE

Although partly trained fans can be bought, it is possible to create your own. Plant a two-year-old peach or nectarine between late autumn and mid-winter, about 20–23 cm (8–9 in) from a wall (soil close to a wall will become dry very quickly in summer). Erect tiers of supporting wires, positioned 7.5–10 cm (3–4 in) from the wall and about 23 cm (9 in) apart. The lowest wire needs to be about 38 cm (15 in) above the soil.

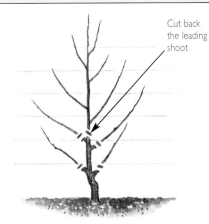

Cut back the leading shoot

1 In late winter, cut back the leading shoot to about 60 cm (2 ft) above the ground and slightly above a healthy growth bud. In addition, cut back all of the sideshoots to one bud from their base.

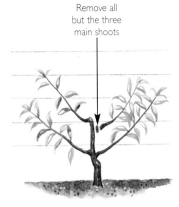

Remove all but the three main shoots

2 By early summer, shoots will have developed. Cut off all but the top one and two others lower down and, preferably, opposite each other. It is these lower ones that will form the main and lower arms of the fan.

PLANTING AND PRUNING A FAN-TRAINED PEACH OR NECTARINE (CONT.)

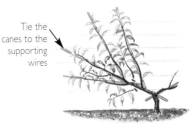

Tie the canes to the supporting wires

3 In mid-summer, cut off the central stem just above the two arms and tie them to two bamboo canes; tie the canes to the wires, keeping them at an angle of about 45°.

4 In early spring of the following year, just as growth is beginning, cut each of the two arms back to a growth bud or a triple bud, 30–45 cm (12–18 in) from the main, central stem.

5 During summer, choose four shoots on each arm. The first will extend growth; two on the top side of the arm will create further arms, as will one on the underside. Cut back all other shoots to leave one leaf. Tie these arms to canes.

Cut back the arms to downward-pointing growth buds

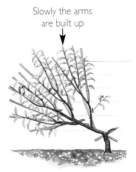

Slowly the arms are built up

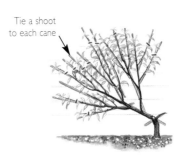

Tie a shoot to each cane

6 During late winter of the following year, cut back each of the arms to about one-third of the growth made during the previous year, cutting each of them to a downward-pointing growth bud.

7 In the following summer, let growth continue from the ends of the arms and allow three new sideshoots to develop on each of them. Tie them to canes. Preferably, these new shoots should be spaced about 10 cm (4 in) apart on the upper and lower sides of the arms.

8 In late summer, the laterals selected earlier in the year will be 38–45 cm (15–18 in) long. Pinch out the growing tip of each shoot and tie them to canes. These shoots will bear fruits during the following year.

9 During the following late spring – and in subsequent years – completely cut out shoots that are growing towards or away from the wall. If they have flower buds at their bases, cut them to two leaves long. Young shoots that developed in the previous year will bear fruits during the current season; they will bear blossom as well as young shoots by early summer. At the base of each of these young shoots, choose one sideshoot (which later will form a replacement shoot), another in the middle (this will act as a reserve replacement shoot) and one at the tip that will extend growth. Pinch back the remaining sideshoots to two leaves from their bases. Later, when both the replacement shoot (and the reserve one) are 38–45 cm (15–18 in) long, nip out the growing points on each of them. Later, when fruits have been picked, cut back each lateral that produced fruits to the replacement shoot. However, if the replacement shoot has become damaged, or is not vigorous, cut back to the reserve shoot. During subsequent years, repeat this technique, endeavouring to encourage the development of fresh shoots each year that will bear fruits during the following year.

Thinning congested fruits

Thinning the fruits is essential if the crop is heavy. Start thinning them when they are the size of large peas and stop when they reach the size of walnuts. Thin fan-trained peaches to leave fruits (after the final thinning) 23 cm (9 in) apart, and nectarines 15 cm (6 in). With bush forms, fruits can be left slightly closer together.

Raspberries

How should I prune my raspberries?

There are two types of these popular summer fruits: summer-fruiting raspberries bear fruits during mid-summer and continue to the early part of late summer, while autumn-fruiting types bear fruits from the latter part of late summer to the first frosts of autumn. Each of these types requires a different pruning technique. However, they both need support, usually from tiered wires strained between strong posts and aligned north to south.

PLANTING AND PRUNING

Plant bare-rooted raspberry canes in early winter or early spring. Container-grown types can be planted at any time of the year when the weather and soil are suitable. Plant them slightly deeper than the level at which they were growing in the container. This applies to both summer- and autumn-fruiting types. Space canes 38–45 cm (15–18 in) apart in rows 1.5–1.8 m (5–6 ft) apart.

Summer-fruiting raspberries are easy to grow and pruning is not complicated.

AUTUMN-FRUITING RASPBERRIES

These develop fruits on shoots produced during the same season. Therefore, pruning is quite simple: during late winter, cut all canes to within 5 cm (2 in) of the soil. This encourages the development of young canes that will later bear fruits.

PRUNING SUMMER-FRUITING RASPBERRIES

Prune newly planted canes

Later, these are cut to soil level

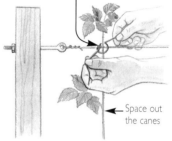

Use soft string to tie the canes loosely but securely to the wires

Space out the canes

1 Immediately after planting, cut all canes to 23–30 cm (9–12 in) high. In spring, plants start to produce young canes that will bear fruits during the following year. At this stage, cut off to soil level each cane which was left 23–30 cm (9–12 in) high at planting time. Do not prune the new canes.

2 As the canes grow, tie them to the wires. In late winter of the following year cut off their tops about 15 cm (6 in) above the top wire. These are the canes that will later bear fruits during the same year.

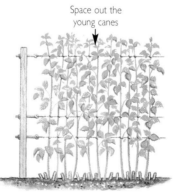

Space out the young canes

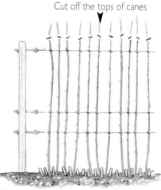

Cut off the tops of canes

3 After the fruits have been picked, cut to soil level all canes that produced fruits. Additionally, space out and tie in to the wires all new canes. These will bear fruits during the following year.

4 During each subsequent year, in late winter cut off the tops of all canes to 15 cm (6 in) above the top wire. Then, after the fruits have been picked, cut out all fruited shoots to soil level and tie in the new canes to the supporting wires.

Blackberries, hybrid berries and loganberries

Cultivated forms of blackberries produce sweeter and plumper fruits than their wild cousins, the brambles. Hybrid berries are mainly crosses between blackberries and raspberries and include Tayberries, Boysenberries and Dewberries. Most are not as vigorous as blackberries. Loganberries are said to have originated in North America where Judge J.H. Logan spotted a cross between a raspberry and a blackberry. They all bear fruits on canes.

Do I need to prune my blackberries every year?

PLANTING

Plant bare-rooted blackberry, hybrid berry and loganberry canes in early winter or early spring. Container-grown types can be planted at any time of the year when the weather and soil are suitable. Plant them slightly deeper than before.

Space canes 1.8–3 m (6–10 ft) apart in rows with 1.8 m (6 ft) between them. Provide a supporting framework of tiered wires strained between posts. Position the wires 90 cm (3 ft), 1.2 m (4 ft), 1.5 m (5 ft) and 1.8 m (6 ft) above the soil.

PRUNING BLACKBERRIES, HYBRID BERRIES AND LOGANBERRIES

After planting, prune the canes

I Immediately after being planted, cut down all canes to about 23 cm (9 in) above the soil. Sever them slightly above a strong, healthy bud. Each year, plants will produce new canes. Therefore, in any one year plants will have canes that are bearing fruits, and new canes that will produce fruits during the following year. Always wear gloves, as the canes are mostly very thorny.

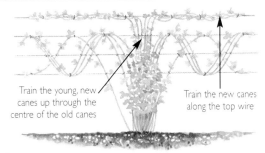

Train the young, new canes up through the centre of the old canes

Train the new canes along the top wire

3 In the second year, train the new canes up through the centre of the plant and along the top wire. In autumn, after the fruits have been picked, cut out to their base all canes that produced fruits during that season.

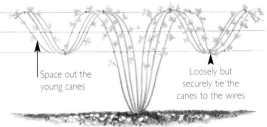

Space out the young canes

Loosely but securely tie the canes to the wires

2 During the first summer, young canes grow from the plant's base and these will bear fruits during the following year. At this stage, all that is necessary is to weave and train the young canes along the wires. However, at this stage leave the top wire free from canes.

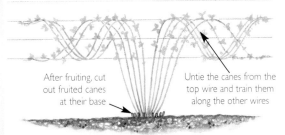

After fruiting, cut out fruited canes at their base

Untie the canes from the top wire and train them along the other wires

4 Immediately after cutting out the fruited canes, untie the new ones from the top wire and space them out over the other wires, but leave the top wire free for young canes that will be produced in the following year. During subsequent years, all that is needed is to repeat this sequence of cutting out fruited canes, and spreading out and tying in young ones produced during the same season.

Blackcurrants

What is the pruning technique for blackcurrants?

Blackcurrants are popular fruits because they are easy to grow and prune. Plants eventually form large bushes, with stems growing directly from soil level or near the plant's base. This method of growing is known as 'stooling' (see page 7), and pruning established plants involves cutting out to their bases old shoots which have borne fruits. This is performed immediately the fruits are picked and encourages the development of fresh shoots that later bear fruits.

Blackcurrants are relatively easy to prune, and this should be carried out as soon as the fruits have been picked.

PLANTING AND PRUNING

Plant bare-rooted plants during their dormant period, from late autumn to late winter or early spring. Container-grown ones can be planted whenever the weather and soil allow. Space the bushes about 1.5 m (5 ft) apart. Do not congest the bushes.

Renovation

When neglected, bushes become a tangled mass of old wood that bears few and inferior fruits. Dig up and replace very old bushes, but if neglect has been for only 3–4 years cut all stems to their bases in late summer or early autumn. This means that plants will not bear fruits during the following season; in subsequent years, cut out all wood that produced fruits. Additionally, give a boost to growth by sprinkling a general fertilizer around bushes in spring. Thoroughly soak the soil with water and keep it moist for several months.

PRUNING BARE-ROOTED BUSHES

1 Plant bare-rooted bushes during their dormant period, positioning them slightly deeper than before – the previous soil-level mark can be seen on the stem. Firm soil over and around the roots and immediately cut all stems to about 2.5 cm (1 in) above the soil.

2 By the end of the following summer, shoots will have developed. Do not prune them, as they will bear fruits during the following year. In autumn, leaves will fall from these shoots.

3 After the fruits have been picked during the following year, use secateurs to cut out to their bases all shoots that produced fruits. At the same time, cut out damaged and crossing shoots. In subsequent years, prune bushes in the same way.

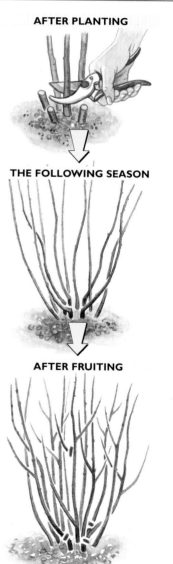

AFTER PLANTING

THE FOLLOWING SEASON

AFTER FRUITING

Red- and whitecurrants

These types of currant bear fruits on short spurs developed on the old wood, as well as in clusters at the bases of young growths formed during the previous year. Both red- and whitecurrants are usually grown as bushes, each with a short 'leg', about 15–20 cm (6–8 in) long, that links the framework of shoots to the roots. Sometimes, they are also grown as cordons, against either a strong stake or a framework of supporting wires.

How should I prune red- and whitecurrants?

PLANTING AND PRUNING BUSH-GROWN PLANTS

This is the easiest way to grow red- and whitecurrants, and does not involve stakes or supporting wires. Plant bare-rooted plants in late autumn or early winter, or in late winter or early spring. Plant container-grown plants whenever the soil and weather allow. Space the bushes about 1.5 m (5 ft) apart.

REDCURRANTS AS CORDONS

Step 1 ~ In winter, plant bare-rooted, one-year-old plants in a line, spacing them 38 cm (15 in) apart. Immediately shorten the central shoot to half its length, and cut lateral shoots to one bud from their base. Completely remove sideshoots within 10 cm (4 in) of the ground. Stake each plant.

Step 2 ~ During the early part of mid-summer, cut back the current season's sideshoots to 4–5 leaves from their base. At this stage, do not prune the top of the central stem, but make sure it is firmly supported.

Step 3 ~ During the following winter, cut the central, leading shoot to a bud that leaves about 15 cm (6 in) of new growth. Also cut back lateral shoots that were pruned during mid-summer to leave 2.5 cm (1 in) of new growth. In later years, cut leading shoots back to leave 2.5 cm (1 in) of new growth.

Step 4 ~ During the following summer – and all subsequent ones – leave the pruning of the leading shoot until winter, but cut back sideshoots during summer to leave 4–5 leaves of fresh growth. Continue to tie in the leading shoot to the cane.

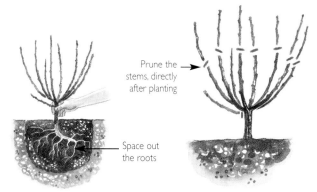

Prune the stems, directly after planting

Space out the roots

1 Plant a two- or three-year-old bush, spacing out the roots in the hole and planting slightly deeper than before. The old soil-level mark can be seen on the stem. Ensure that the 'leg' remains; firm soil over the roots.

2 Immediately after planting, cut the main shoots back by a half. This initial pruning encourages strong growth. Also cut sideshoots back to the main shoots. The illustration here shows a three-year-old bush.

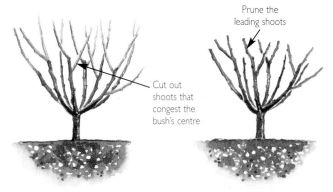

Cut out shoots that congest the bush's centre

Prune the leading shoots

3 During the following winter, cut out shoots that cross the plant's centre. At the same time, cut back sideshoots that are not needed to develop into main shoots. Also cut back leading shoots by about a half.

4 During the following years, it is only necessary to cut back the leading shoots by about 2.5 cm (1 in). Cut back lateral shoots to form new spurs, and remove old shoots that are causing congestion.

Gooseberries

Like red- and whitecurrants, gooseberry bushes must be grown on a short 'leg', 15–20 cm (6–8 in) long, that links the framework of shoots to the roots. Gooseberries are borne on one-year-old wood and spurs that develop from the older shoots. Initial pruning creates a strong framework of permanent branches, while later it is used to continue the development of fruiting spurs. Gooseberries can also be grown as cordons.

PLANTING AND PRUNING GOOSEBERRIES

Plant bare-rooted plants in late autumn or early winter, or in late winter or early spring. Plant container-grown plants whenever the soil and weather allow. Space the bushes 1.2–1.5 m (4–5 ft) apart.

Shorten young shoots

1 Plant a one-year-old gooseberry bush during its dormant period. Form a hole that is large enough to accommodate the roots and position the plant so that it is slightly deeper than before; a dark mark on the stem gives an indication about the previous depth. Spread and evenly firm soil over and around the roots. Immediately after planting, prune back each main branch by about a half, cutting to an upward-pointing bud.

2 By the following late autumn or early winter, the bush will have developed a strong framework. Shorten back by about a half all shoots produced during the year, cutting to upward-pointing buds. Also remove suckers and cut out low stems.

Prune lateral shoots

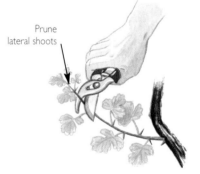

4 During the latter part of early summer, prune lateral shoots produced during that season to five leaves. At this stage, do not prune the leader shoots. Later, during winter, cut back the leader shoots by half, and all lateral shoots to two buds from their base. Subsequently, repeat this summer- and winter-pruning regime.

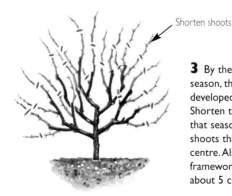

Shorten shoots

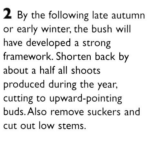

3 By the end of the following season, the bush will have developed further shoots. Shorten those produced during that season by a half, and cut out shoots that crowd the plant's centre. Also shorten non-framework lateral shoots to about 5 cm (2 in) long.

THINNING THE FRUITS

The size of dessert fruits can be increased by thinning them in early summer – pinch off every other berry. The berries that are removed can be used for bottling or as a filling for pies.

Figs

Figs were favoured by the Romans and widely planted by them some 2,000 years ago. This succulent fruit thrives in sub-tropical regions. It also grows well in warm, temperate climates and especially when planted as a fan against a warm, sunny wall. The fruits ripen between late summer and mid-autumn and are borne on the tips of well-ripened shoots produced during the previous season. It is essential that the roots are constricted.

Can I grow a fig tree against a wall?

PLANTING AND PRUNING

Plant container-grown figs in late winter or early spring, against a wall and spaced 3.6–4.5 m (12–15 ft) apart. The roots of figs must be constricted to prevent plants developing excessive, leafy growth at the expense of fruits. Prepare the planting position by digging a hole about 90 cm (3 ft) square and deep. Line the hole with paving slabs or bricks and fill the base with 23 cm (9 in) of clean rubble. Top up the hole with a mixture of soil, small pieces of rubble and a dusting of bonemeal. An alternative way is to use a large pot, 38–45 cm (15–18 in) wide, and to sink it into the ground, with its rim protruding slightly above the surrounding soil.

The very popular 'Brown Turkey' produces figs that are ready for picking during late summer and early autumn.

PLANTING AND PRUNING FIGS

1 In winter, plant a two-year-old container-grown fig in the hole and 15–20 cm (6–8 in) from the wall. Remove the plant from its container and position it 10 cm (4 in) deeper than before. Firm soil around the roots. Erect tiers of wires, 23 cm (9 in) apart, starting from 45 cm (18 in) above the ground and finishing at the top of the wall. In spring, cut the central stem to just above the lowest wire and directly above a lateral shoot. Select two shoots, on each side of the plant, to form the 'arms' and tie each of them to a cane secured at 45° to the wires. Also cut back both arms to a bud about 45 cm (18 in) from the main stem, and cut off all other lateral shoots.

2 During the following summer, allow four shoots to grow from each of the two arms. On each arm, one shoot will extend its growth, with another shoot on the lower side and two on the upper side. Rub out all other buds growing from the arms and tie the eight shoots to bamboo canes, themselves tied to the tiers of supporting wires.

3 In late winter of the following year, use sharp secateurs to cut back each of the main shoots. Cut them to slightly above a bud that will continue growth in the desired direction and create a fan. Leave about 60 cm (2 ft) of the previous season's growth. In the following summer, rub out unwanted buds that would create growth and cause congestion.

4 Once the framework is formed, routine pruning is needed in spring and summer. In spring, cut out frost-damaged and diseased shoots, and all shoots growing either towards or out from the wall. Also thin out young shoots to just above one bud from their base. In early summer, cut back young growths to five leaves from their base. These develop into fruiting shoots for the following year.

Outdoor grape vines

Do grapes grow well in temperate climates?

Grapes have been grown for more than 5,000 years and it is claimed that civilization spread with the advent of grape-growing and wine-making. Grapes were grown outdoors in northern Europe in Roman times, but cold weather later made this difficult. The global climate is now improving, making outdoor grapes more successful in temperate areas. Pruning is relatively simple, encouraging a balance between new growth and development of fruiting spurs.

HOW TO GROW OUTDOOR GRAPES

There are many ways to grow grape vines, but for outdoor cultivation the 'single cordon' method is the simplest and easiest to perform. Tiers of 10-gauge galvanized wires strained between posts are essential. Position them against a warm wall, spacing them 30 cm (12 in) apart and held about 10–13 cm (4–5 in) away from the wall. The lowest wire needs to be 45 cm (18 in) above the soil, with the top one about 2.1 m (7 ft) high. A strong framework of wires is essential.

PLANTING AND PRUNING OUTDOOR GRAPES

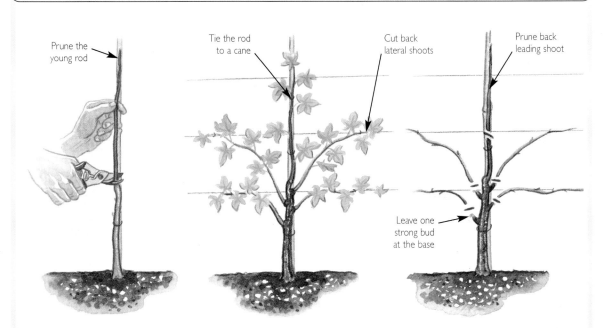

Prune the young rod

Tie the rod to a cane

Cut back lateral shoots

Prune back leading shoot

Leave one strong bud at the base

1 Plant bare-rooted grape vines in late autumn or early winter, or in late winter or early spring. Space the plants 1.5 m (5 ft) apart in rows. Immediately after being planted, cut the main stem 50–60 cm (20–24 in) above the soil and slightly above a strong, healthy bud. Prune all other shoots to one bud from their base. Tie the rod to a cane, which itself is tied to the wires.

2 During the following summer, a shoot will grow from the top of the rod, as well as from buds lower down. Tie the central stem upright and to a cane. In mid-summer, use sharp secateurs to cut back the lateral shoots (those that originate from buds on the side of the rod) to just beyond 5–6 leaves. Also cut back to one leaf all shoots that are growing from these laterals, and cut out shoots growing from the rod's base.

3 In the following winter, cut back the leading shoot, leaving about one-third of the growth produced during the previous year. Additionally, cut back all lateral shoots to leave just one strong bud at the base of young shoots produced during the previous summer. Later, these will create further growth.

PLANTING AND PRUNING OUTDOOR GRAPES (CONTINUED)

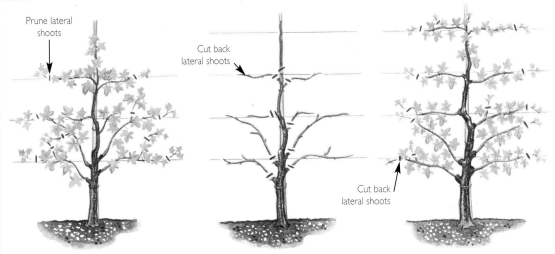

Prune lateral shoots

Cut back lateral shoots

Cut back lateral shoots

4 During the following summer, when lateral shoots have produced about 10 leaves, cut them back to 5–6 leaves from their base. Pinch out sub-lateral shoots to one leaf from their base. To conserve the plant's energies, nip out flower trusses that may form on the lateral shoots.

5 Between early and mid-winter, cut back the leading shoot to leave about one-third of the new growth that was produced during the previous summer. Additionally, cut back lateral shoots to leave just one bud on the new growth.

6 During the following summer, cut back lateral shoots that have a flower truss to two leaves beyond the fruiting cluster. Laterals that are not bearing fruits should be pruned to just beyond 5–6 leaves. Pinch back to one leaf shoots that are developing from lateral shoots.

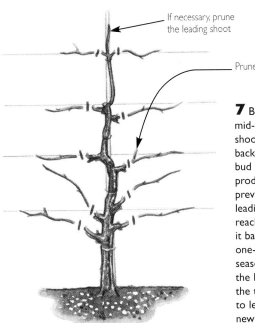

If necessary, prune the leading shoot

Prune lateral shoots

7 Between early and mid-winter, prune lateral shoots by cutting them back to the first strong bud on the growth produced during the previous year. If the leading shoot has not reached the top wire, cut it back to leave about one-third of the previous season's growth. When the leading shoot reaches the top wire, cut it back to leave just two buds of new growth.

THINNING GRAPES

To enable grapes to grow to their full size, thin the bunches as soon as the individual berries start to swell. Over a couple of weeks – and using a pair of long, pointed scissors – snip out small fruits. As well as giving individual grapes more space, thinning helps to ensure a good circulation of air around the fruits, preventing the onset of plant-debilitating diseases.

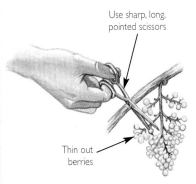

Use sharp, long, pointed scissors

Thin out berries

8 During the following years, the objective of pruning is encourage the development of young lateral shoots that will bear fruits. Prune back the laterals and sub-laterals in both summer and winter, as described and illustrated in steps 6 and 7 (see above).

If thinning is neglected, the best possible fruits will not be produced. Take care that you do not damage the remaining fruits.

Glossary

Anvil secateurs Type of secateurs where a cutting blade cuts against a firm, metal surface.

Bark-ringing The removal of a narrow strip of bark from around part of the trunk of an apple or pear tree to encourage fruiting. It was earlier used on large trees, but with the introduction of dwarf and moderately vigorous rootstocks it is now seldom used. Do not bark-ring cherry, plum, gage, nectarine or peach trees.

Biennial bearing The tendency of some apple varieties to produce more or fewer fruits during one year than during another.

Bleeding The loss of sap from a cut surface. If pruning is performed at the wrong time, some plants freely exude sap.

Blossom bud Sometimes known as a fruit bud, it is much fatter than a vegetative bud, the role of which is to continue growth rather than to develop into a fruit.

Bole The trunk of a tree, from ground level to the lowest branch.

Bow saw Large saw with a strong, metal frame. It is ideal for cutting thick branches. It cuts on the push stroke.

Breastwood Shoots which grow outwards from woody plants. They do not contribute to the plant's growth, nor to its beauty. They need to be cut out cleanly at their point of origin.

Bush A woody plant where there is only a short stem between the ground and the lowest branch. Also refers to soft fruits such as blackcurrants, which have a mass of stems at ground level, and to red- and whitecurrants, as well as gooseberries, which have a short 'leg' between the soil and lowest shoots.

Bypass secateurs Type of secateurs where one blade crosses the other. Earlier known as parrot-type or cross-over secateurs.

Callus Hard, protective tissue which forms over a cut or wounded surface.

Cane fruits Plants such as raspberries, blackberries and hybrid berries which have cane-like stems that grow from ground level.

Central leader The central, dominant and vertical stem on a plant.

Conifers A group of shrubs and trees, usually evergreen but several are deciduous, which often bear needle-like or narrow leaves.

Cordon A fruit tree (usually an apple or pear tree), although it can be a soft fruit such as a red- or whitecurrant, that is trained and pruned to form one, two, three or four stems. Mostly, they are grown at a 45-degree angle, although some are upright.

Crown The main branch system on a tree.

Deadheading The removal of dead flowers to prevent the development of seeds.

Deciduous Describes a plant that each year sheds its leaves in autumn and develops a fresh set during the following spring.

Dieback The death of tips of shoots, often the result of severe frost, faulty pruning and, occasionally, damage from pests and diseases.

Dormant period The resting period, usually autumn and winter, when a plant makes little or no growth. Many plants, such as apples and pears, are pruned during this period.

Espalier A fruit tree trained so that its branches form tiers, usually supported by a framework of wires.

Evergreen Describes a plant which appears to retain its foliage throughout the year. However, these plants continually shed leaves and develop others.

Eye A bud on a rose.

Fan A fruit tree trained so that its branches create the shape of a fan.

Feathered Describes a maiden tree with a few lateral shoots arising directly from the main stem.

Fruit bud Also known as a blossom bud; it is fatter than a growth bud, and develops into a flower followed by a fruit.

Grecian saw Type of pruning saw with a curved, tapering blade that cuts on the pull stroke.

Growing point The extreme tip of shoots or roots.

Half-standard A tree with a stem (trunk) 75 cm–1.2 m (2½–4 ft) long between the ground and the lowest branch.

Hand pruners North American term for secateurs.

Hedging shears Used to trim hedges as well as ericaceous plants. Some shears have a notch at the bases of the blades and these enable thicker stems to be cut.

Lateral A shoot that grows directly from a main branch or stem.

Leader The leading shoot or main growth part of a branch. With a one-year-old tree, this is a single shoot, but older trees will have several branches and each of them will have a leading shoot.

Leg A short stem – on a gooseberry, red- or whitecurrant – between the roots and the lowest stem.

Loppers Long-handled secateurs, used to cut thick shoots. They have either a bypass or an anvil cutting action.

Maiden tree A one-year-old tree, formed of a single stem and without sideshoots.

Nipping out The removal of the tip of a shoot to encourage the development of sideshoots.

Parrot secateurs An early name for bypass or cross-over secateurs, where one blade crosses another.

Partial evergreen Describes some shrubs, such as *Ligustrum ovalifolium* (common privet), that remain evergreen in most climates, but in cold winters may lose their leaves.

Pleaching Training and pruning a line of trees planted close together to form a 'hedge' at their top. The lower part of each tree is bare of branches, but at head height and above they are interlaced.

Pollarding Cutting back the main branches on a tree to near the top of the trunk.

Powerbreaker A device that instantly cuts off power to mains-powered electric equipment should a fault occur. It is an essential piece of equipment to install when using electrical hedge-trimmers or chainsaws.

Pruning Severing of parts of a tree, shrub or climber to restrict and regulate growth, to shape or promote the development of flowers, stems and fruits.

Root-pruning Severing of the roots on a tree to reduce its vigour and encourage fruiting.

Shrub A woody plant with several shoots arising from ground level. Some plants can be grown as a tree or a shrub, depending on initial pruning and training.

Spur A short, lateral shoot which bears flowers and fruit buds. Pruning is performed to encouraged their development.

Stooling Cutting trees or shrubs down to near soil level – or close to it – to encourage the development of young shoots. These can be used when budding or grafting fruit trees. Alternatively, some ornamental shrubs and trees are pruned annually to encourage the development of young, colourful stems.

Stopping The removal of the tip of a shoot to encourage the development of sideshoots.

Sub-lateral A shoot which grows from a lateral shoot.

Sucker A shoot which grows from a stem or root of a grafted or budded plant, below the position where the varietal part and rootstock were united. On bush roses they grow from the roots, and on standard types from the stem.

Thinning The removal of fruiting spurs or fruits so that the remaining ones have more space, light and air in which to develop.

Topiary The art of training and clipping evergreen shrubs to form distinctive shapes.

Tree A woody plant with a permanently clear stem between the branches and the ground.

Trunk The woody structure between the roots and the branches. Some trees are half-standards, while others are full standards.

Water-shoots Shoots that grow on the trunks of trees, often from points at which stems and branches were earlier cut off.

Wound paint Special paint, usually including a fungicide, used to coat pruning cuts to encourage healing and to prevent the entry of disease.

Index